all about parties

all about parties

by edith gilbert

PUBLISHED BY
HEARTHSIDE PRESS, INC.,
NEW YORK, NEW YORK 10016

ACKNOWLEDGMENTS

The most pleasant part of authoring a book arrives at this moment when one is privileged to say "Thank You" to all the wonderful people who helped make this book possible. There is Eleanor Ratigan, a writer who inspired my earliest efforts; there is Ray Shaw, a painstaking cook who meticulously measured and kitchen-tested each recipe for me; there is Nedda Anders, Editor of Hearthside, who skillfully pointed the way to achievement; there are friends—too numerous to mention—who've shared ideas and experiences; and finally, there's my tolerant husband who has been inconvenienced beyond measure. To each—my deepest gratitude.

Contents

Contents

1

Key to Successful Entertaining

The more, the merrier; the fewer, the better fare.

Old Proverb

My favorite parties are those filled with delightful memories of people, of lights and glitter, delicate fragrances, of warmth and love and kindnesses. Some of my favorite parties have been huge affairs with the correct number of guests per square foot, with cold drinks and hot music, where it's fun striking up a conversation unexpectedly with someone whose passion for a particular play, or Imperial jade, or a fast game of tennis, is as great as one's own.

Then again, sometimes my favorite parties run small because here I can chat with all those interesting people one never has the chance to enjoy at large affairs. At intimate coteries I can sit down and listen to people exchange ideas instead of merely information; where a wise woman asks an intelligent man, "What do you think?" instead of telling him what she thinks; where contacts are made—not exploited; where small talk, spiced with wit, is appreciated and not considered a waste of time.

IT'S THE SMALL TOUCH THAT COUNTS

These memorable, magical parties, both large and small, don't just happen, and we'll tell *you* why chapter by chapter. One of the keys to successful party giving is not so much *what* is served but *how* it's served!

Let me recount an incident that took place on a yacht where I overheard the steward ask a guest if he'd like something hot or cold to drink.

"Something cold."

"Hard or soft?"

"Just a plain glass of water, please," came the reply.

"Vichy, Polin or Mountain Valley Water, sir?" pressed the steward.

"Plain water," sighed the visitor.

In a jiffy the steward returned. "Anything else?" he inquired as he offered a clear glass of cold water beside a folded monogrammed napkin on a silver tray. And floating on top of the water was a paper-thin slice of lemon, proving that it's quite possible to serve a plain, cold glass of water with as much flair as a chilled bowl of caviar!

Now when the postman rings *your* doorbell on a hot summer day and you offer him a glass of water with a thin slice of lemon, he may think you're some kind of kook, but the ladies at next week's canasta game will vote you as the hostess with the mostes' on the block.

SOME HOSTESSES ARE FUSSY—
AND SOME ARE FLEXIBLE!

Chances are your block sports two kinds of hostesses, just like my block does. First, there's the nervous hostess who keeps all her possessions wrapped in cellophane (she even has slip covers for her slip covers!) and she never removes the cellophane from her lamp shades. If she allows you into her home, she sits like a watch-bird and *watches* every move you make! She's always checking to see that no one drips or spills, scratches or burns, creases or musses anything. She regiments her guests, and people don't have much fun here.

Then there's the second kind of hostess. She also takes pride in her surroundings, but she never loses sight of the fact that her home and its furnishings are meant for the enjoyment and comfort of *people,* and she doesn't allow herself to become the slave of inanimate objects. She enjoys entertaining even at the last minute. She entertains whether she has help or not, whether the house is full of children or not, whether this year's income is up or down. She is flexible and manages to shift the scene, expand the menu, cut corners and still come up with a memorable evening. Because she's confident, relaxed and poised, she enjoys herself whenever or wherever she entertains.

Speaking of being relaxed and poised always reminds me of this classic story that happened at a small dinner party in Shanghai, China many years ago. During dinner the waiter approached the dining table carrying a beautifully garnished goose on a silver platter. He tripped and the goose slipped to the floor. Calmly Madame turned to him and said, "Boy, bring in the other one!" Naturally most of the guests were pretty certain there was no "other" goose in the kitchen. Yet, after the bird was brought around a second time, everyone tactfully raved how delicious the *other* goose tasted. Well, who knows? Perhaps there was another goose in the oven?

HOW TO BE AN EXECUTIVE'S WIFE

According to one of the top management consulting firms in the country, playing it cool is the key to success in our space age just as it was in the pioneer age; a wife is money in the bank and good ones open the path to top executive positions.

But there's no one road to success as an executive's wife! Mainly, she is someone who is at home in different social situations. The gorgeous creatures dripping in furs and jewels, who dance through our society pages today are often the same "jewels" who whip up a fondue tomorrow at that little ski hideaway or who prepare a platter of tantalizing hors d'oeuvre in the poolhouse kitchen or plan a benefit dinner for a thousand people, or are top-flight business executives themselves. With the help situation what it is today, a woman needs to know how to prepare for company in a pinch or to tell someone when to put the roast in the oven. When she engages a cateress for special occasions, she needs to know how to get the best out of her. This know-how is invaluable to the red-carpet, successful social life.

Let's assume for a moment that a successful social life is half the secret of a man's business success. But what exactly is a successful social life? Do we need to suffer through a stretch of stuffy, formal functions? Heavens no! All we mean by a successful social life is to have friends with whom one shares one's home, one's time and one's interest in a congenial, pleasant atmosphere. Ever since Eleanor Roosevelt served hot dogs to the king and queen of England, Old World formality flew right out the White House window and the free-wheeling American hostess with her natural charm and lighthearted manner has come into her attractive own.

BUDGET YOUR TIME AND ENERGY

With her automatic dishwasher, blender, rotisserie, freezer, the executive wife accomplishes miracles in her compact kitchen. She knows how to save time and energy. But all too many homemakers forget that savings are meant to be spent! A slice of time saved by automation is profitably spent in leisure activities—a morning coffee, a stimulating afternoon tea, a jolly evening of cards, a gay dinner party or a glittering dance.

Naturally it takes a sense of balance to budget one's time and energy; to find energy for things that are important and things we enjoy. Budget time for cleaning, marketing, cooking—yes, but budget time for rest? Too many homemakers forget that this important consideration should come first. When one is overtired, it's easy to be crotchety and impatient with those around us. Let washing curtains go another week if it means giving up your rest period. Your devoted friends are coming over to enjoy your sparkling face, not your sparkling curtains!

Of course, the best stimulant to energy is happiness. Thomas Wolfe said, "There's no spectacle on earth more appealing than a beautiful woman in the act of cooking dinner for someone she loves!" The corollary of this statement is: don't be pushed into giving a party for people you don't like! We all know things (and people) that make us unhappy, angry, or fearful. When energy is directed towards battling hostile elements, there's little left for the job at hand. On the other hand, if you look forward to entertaining . . . if you think that you are giving a fun party . . . you'll find plenty of time to get everything done.

A trick to relieve the monotony of any job is to think up ways of improving it. How to give a prettier, livelier, more amusing party might be the answer for those who find entertaining a monotonous chore.

THE PARTY PRICE TAGS NEED NOT SHOW

And while we're on the subject of budgeting our time and energy, let's take a minute to talk about budgeting the cost of our entertaining (Chapter VI too). All of us, I'm sure, entertain simply at times and splurge at other times, but simple entertaining to one person may mean splurging to someone else. When in doubt, remember this rule—it's better to serve a tasty stew than a tough steak! The magic ingredient of a swinging party has never been an unlimited $ budget. We've all been to dull, duller, the dullest parties that have cost, cost, cost!

When we talk of budgets, let us remember we're talking in comparative terms. Inviting friends for brunch is ordinarily less costly than having friends for dinner—unless of course, you plan to serve fresh caviar and imported champagne for brunch! Entertaining at home, if you prepare the meal yourself, is a lot less expensive than if dining and wining your friends in an elegant restaurant or club. Making your own invitations is not only less expensive but often more fun than having them engraved. Renting equipment may be more budget-wise than buying something you'll never use again. Hiring a caterer may be more economical for some people than keeping full-time help.

TO MARKET TO MARKET TO BUY A FAT PIG!

People always ask about quantities. Here are a few basic principles that I follow when marketing for a party, but age, sex, and weather are variables. For example, people eat more outdoors than in; heavy drinkers eat less than light drinkers. When planning a cookout for young men and women, double the quantity. For college athletes, triple the quantity. For a ladies luncheon, reduce the quantity.

Hors d'oeuvres: Allow 3 pieces each or 1/8 pound sea food such as shelled shrimp, crab meat, lobster, etc.

Main course: Allow a full 1/4 pound boneless meat such as hamburger, cubed beef etc. per person. Meat with bone, allow 1/2 to 1 pound, depending on amount of bone.

Cooked potatoes, rice, vegetables, etc.: Allow a minimum of 1/3 cup per person, or 1 medium whole vegetable as cooked potato, baked tomato, etc.

Coffee: One pound coffee and 2 gallons water equals 40 to 48 servings.

Tea: One pound loose tea equals 150 servings.

MIX-AND-MATCH MENUS AND RECIPES

We've tried in the following chapters to give you enough variations so that you can mix-and-match your party menus and decorations to suit your particular and personal requirements and the requirements of your budget too, whatever it may be!

You'll notice as you read along that oodles of our recipes are mix and matchable too. For instance, if you keep on serving omelets and crepes at eleven P.M. you may be Mrs. Dullsville— why not the same fare for a Sunday morning brunch? Steak tartare attracts a man's eye as readily for lunch as for hors d'oeuvre; many appetizers do as well on the tea table as on the cocktail table; green spinach salad with anchovies blends as smoothly with roast beef as with cheese fondue; and our Bundt Kuchen recipe and Pecan Rolls could truly be called the basics in a trousseau of recipes.

We hope you won't feel bound by any hard and fast rules as you experiment with a few of our suggestions, instead, you'll perhaps find it easier in future to coordinate a menu with a party theme whereby you'll create a mood, a style and a personality so completely your own, people will say, "That party is *you*"— but not a monotonous *you!*

BORROWING—A MIXED BLESSING

Once in awhile most people need to rent or borrow an extra card table, a few chairs or a coffee maker when entertaining a large group. Although we much prefer renting it's not always possible, especially in small communities where there are no rental facilities. We've faced this reality throughout the book, frequently referring to borrowing equipment of various kinds in spite of Shakespeare's solid good advice, "Neither a borrower nor lender be; for loan oft loses both itself and friends."

Certainly there are some things we never want to risk loaning and surely it's our privilege to say so. One might easily say something like this, "No, I just can't let you borrow this crystal punch bowl. It belonged to my grandmother and I'd feel terrible if something happened to it."

If we do decide to make a loan to a friend or neighbor, then let's protect ourselves by making it a habit to put our name on the article we're loaning. Name plates are as old as cookbooks and if we don't have name plates, just jot your name inside the book's cover. Return postage labels printed with your name and address work like charms to bring home stray records, trays, etc. If the label does not stick to the surface, write your name on freezer tape or adhesive tape.

Of course, people who borrow should return the article as soon as possible—preferably the following day, and in perfect condition. Copper and silver should be brightly polished; anything broken or damaged should be repaired or replaced . . . after reporting the accident to the owner.

CASTING A PARTY

My friends were giving me the rundown on a recent dinner party catered in a fashionable home. There were twenty guests, soft lights, good music, imported caviar, fine wines, yet it was as dull as yesterday's headlines.

We wondered why and finally agreed that there are times when a host may turn himself inside out for nothing. The fault lies with the guests.

There are guests who feel that their mere physical presence is all that's required. They arrive promptly. Remove their wraps carefully. Eat quietly. Drink moderately and thank their hosts politely before putting on their things to leave. They feel if they don't spill or break something they're conducting themselves admirably.

But these dullards contribute nothing! They don't listen attentively; they don't smile appreciatively; they don't sigh sympathetically, they don't join eagerly, they don't communicate enthusiastically . . . they just don't!

The trouble with this kind of person is that like a bad apple, he can spoil the whole barrel of fun.

Elizabeth Carpenter, White House press secretary to Mrs. Johnson, sums it up neatly. "For a really good party have on your guest list a few people who make almost a career of going to parties. They're the ones who will turn themselves inside out to make yours go!"

Mrs. Vincent Minelli doesn't invite people to her parties— she casts them! For zest and balance, one needs a variety of personalities including a sprinkling of "doctors, lawyers, Indian chiefs." An architect friend of mine makes it a rule to have people of different ages to his "Thank-God-It's-Friday" cocktail parties. Balance and variety, yes, but the perfect guest list will surely include beautiful women along with men of accomplishment.

A popular guest usually is an experienced party giver who knows it's a treat to be invited to one's home. He'll never "make an appearance" rushing in late from one function and leaving early for the next! (If one must leave early, it's best to thank the hostess in advance and explain why one must leave, then slip out quietly and unobtrusively. In France they call this "taking English leave" and in England it's called "taking French leave" but no matter what it's called, this is a thoughtful way to depart without disrupting a group.)

PARTY PILL IS MY NAME

> I never answer invitations
> I cancel at the last minute
> I telephone a half hour before the party
> I always arrive early—or late
> I like to bring my children and pets
> I don't mingle with the guests
> I monopolize the conversation
> I tell off-color stories
> I make amorous advances
> I enjoy heated, controversial discussions
> I like to drink too much
> I don't want to go home
> I don't write or phone my "thank you's".

Thank God for those precious, lovable guests who may do the most outlandish things but, because of their particular charm, become even more endearing. They're gay—not boisterous; courteous—not fresh; and if they are a little fresh—not obnoxious. They are serious—not somber; they tease—but don't hurt; they're sweet—not gooey; they are sharp—not cutting.

A guest who everlastingly endeared himself to his host way back in 29 B.C. was described by Horace in "A Rich Man Dines." When a canopy fell from the ceiling on the dining room table and the elegant Roman meal was covered with black dust, Balatro complimented his host with the ultimate *bon mot* by saying:

"A host is like a general; adversity reveals his genius, prosperity hides it."

To this the host replied, "Heaven grant you all that you pray for! You are so kind and considerate a guest!"

HOSTESS—WITH APOLOGIES

Of course, guests are not the only pet peeve in this great, big, wide and wonderful world. There are some hostesses I'd gladly nominate for a one-way passage to the moon. Edgar Guest said it first and cleverly:

The Sorry Hostess

She said she was sorry the weather was bad
The night that she asked us to dine;
And she really appeared inexpressibly sad
Because she had hoped 'twould be fine.
She was sorry to hear that my wife had a cold,
And she almost shed tears over that,
And how sorry she was, she most feelingly told,
That the steam wasn't on in the flat.

When the dinner began she apologized twice
For the olives, because they were small;
She was certain the celery, too, wasn't nice,

And the soup didn't suit her at all.
She was sorry she couldn't get whitefish instead
Of the trout that the fishmonger sent,
But she hoped that we'd manage somehow to be fed
Though her dinner was not what she meant.

She spoke her regrets for the salad, and·then
Explained she was really much hurt,
And begged both our pardons again and again
For serving a skimpy dessert.
She was sorry for this and sorry for that,
Though there really was nothing to blame.
And I thought to myself as I put on my hat
Perhaps she is sorry we came.

From—"Just Folks"

INVITATIONS—VERBAL, WRITTEN, LAST MINUTE— BUT SPECIFIC!

Old-fashioned formality reached such extremes during the early nineteenth century that in some Parisian societies if one neglected coming to dinner after having accepted an invitation, one had to forfeit 500 francs or about $10.00.

In today's society, we may be billed after making a reservation at a hotel banquet whether we're there to eat the creamed chicken or not, but generally our social life is much more informal and invitations too are more casual than ever. Herein lies a danger that's reaching significant proportions.

This happened to a friend of mine who invited a casual acquaintance a little too casually for dinner. When her doorbell rang on the appointed day, at the correct time, the hostess almost fainted when she saw her guest dressed in a dinner gown when all she'd planned was a cozy meal with the family!

Inviting someone for a game of cards can become awkward unless one spells out exactly whether one plays for fun or money—and how much. A quarter could easily mean twenty-five cents or a quarter of a cent a point!

Surprises do give a party special appeal—except when it's a fund-raising appeal! It's never in good taste to invite someone to a party and then surprise him by asking for a donation. If the party is given in behalf of charity, this should be clearly stated in the invitation and solicitations should be done by letter or phone the day after.

It's amazing how often people who should know better invite friends while they're at another party or meeting. Sometimes they even rely on a husband to relay the invitation to the wife—a deplorable idea. To avoid misunderstandings, be considerate and follow any casual mention of an invitation with a telephone call. This gives people a chance to circle the date on their home calendar because it's a darn shame holding dinner only to learn that your guests thought they were invited after dinner . . . if they remembered the invitation at all!

Sometimes people are under the false impression that it doesn't make any difference whether they go to a party or not—it's going to be a large affair with lots of people coming and going and their absence won't be noticed. This is untrue. Most hostesses screen their guest list carefully, they do count heads and are disturbed when an expected someone turns into a "no-show"! Often questions are raised: "Did so-and-so say they were coming?" "Shall we call the house?" "Do you think something is wrong?"

Every invitation should be answered "yes" or "no" within a few days. If this is impossible then a call or note of explanation is in order.

When invitations are mailed and one does not receive a reply within a reasonable time, it's best to check why. Perhaps the invited guest is out of town or the invitation has been misaddressed or gone astray.

Of course everyone dreads last-minute cancellations, yet there are times when this too is unavoidable. We bump into Mary hastily filling a prescription in the drug store for her feverish husband and she cries, "We're so disappointed we won't be able to be with you for dinner tomorrow!"

"Horrors," you think. "We need another poker player, but how can I invite someone at the last minute?" Well, why not? Now's the time to call your best friend and be honest, "We're giving a small dinner party tomorrow night and the Plunket's can't come. Will you be a sport and fill in for us?"

Or Jane calls at six o'clock. "Bill's plane is grounded! I'm so sorry he can't be with us tonight." Too late to get a substitute, O.K. But rather than leave an empty place at the table, it's so much more congenial to remove the place setting which only takes a minute. No one likes being seated next to a vacant chair, yet I've seen it happen.

All invitations, verbal or written, should give the exact date, time and place and sometimes dress (black tie, white tie, or blue-jeans). There should be an R.S.V.P. or Please Reply in one corner with a return address or telephone number. One of my pet peeves is to receive an invitation from Mary and Bill or Jane and Tom without a last name. It's thoughtless to make people play "Guess Who?", unless of course you're deliberately planning a Mystery Party!

In addition, one may write when the party is supposed to be over. Open-House from three to five o'clock. Cocktails from five to seven. Tea from two to four o'clock, or whatever one decides. On the phone one might say, "We're having a few friends over for Frank and Dorothy Wednesday evening—it won't be a late evening because they're leaving on an early flight for the South the first thing Thursday morning."

There was a day when it was considered gauche even to have a clock in the living room but those were the days when people knew how long to stay and when to go home. Glenville Kleiser has written these appropriate words on the subject.

The Ideal Hostess—She gleans how long you wish to stay
She lets you go without delay.

The Ideal Guest—She is not difficult to please;
She can be silent as the trees
She shuns all ostentatious show;
She knows exactly when to go.

KEEP AN OPEN HEART—AND TABLE

It's true remaining loyal to old friends is an admirable trait but psychiatrists caution us that in order to keep a healthy mental outlook, we must not become isolated in later life, therefore we must continually make new friends.

While interviewing a moody patient a psychiatrist brought up the subject of friends and asked, "Do you meet new people easily? Are you broadening your circle of friends?"

"Why should I make new friends," replied the cynic, "when I don't like the ones I already have?"

Evidently the Greeks had a healthier mental outlook than the cynic because their definition of the word for guest is Xenos, which also means stranger, making it impossible to translate the friendly American cowboy expression into Greek—be my guest, stranger!

Hospitality is never a matter of inviting the Joneses because we owe them or including a neighbor in order to show off our new carpet. It's more than feeding a crowd or housing a stranger. While listing the intangible gifts of the spirit, the brothers Overstreet (educators, authors, professors) head their list with the Spirit of Hospitality.

"We can welcome our fellow humans when they enter the door of our homes by our manner which says, 'I'm glad you've come. If you feel tired, beset by chores, battered by the demands of life, on the defensive, you can rest here. And you can safely be yourself. If you don't agree, I'll respect your ideas as yours, I won't call them silly or shout you down. Come in . . . be at home. There is room for you here!"

In a home that does more than serve as a hostel, it's possible to schedule as little as one day a week—perhaps on the weekend—when one's table is set with extra loving care, when good china and crystal are given an airing, when dinner is served leisurely, graciously, with thought given to both taste appeal and eye appeal. The French have developed the fine art of eating to its highest degree. Dinner is not only a time to satisfy our hunger, but a form of recreation, a ritual to be enjoyed. Wherever good food, good living and good companions meet they produce what Germans call "Gemütlichkeit". We can't define it but we can experience it!

Creating a pleasant atmosphere at mealtime is not only a matter of aesthetics, but also vital to health. Doctors agree that digestion is definitely improved and appetites stimulated when meals are relaxing. The Bible reminds us, "Better a dry morsel and quietness therewith, than a house full of feasting with strife." (Proverbs 17.1)

It's just a skip and a jump from planning a white tablecloth family dinner to entertaining friends. Then why do we meet with resistance among some people? What's the problem?

In many cases the problem is basically that too many women are unsure, afraid. They worry that their homes are not fine enough or the refreshments won't please or the guests will be bored. Some say it's impossible to entertain until the couch has been recovered or the children are older or the bank account is larger. Excuses, excuses, excuses!

Nor is that all. There are other drawbacks. In some marriages one of the partners is more sociable and out-going than the other. "She" loves to go out for a gay evening or adores having company at home, while "he" couldn't care less! It could be the other way around. "She" is the quiet one who'd rather stay home and watch TV than entertain the boss for dinner. What to do? The solution, as in all successful partnerships, is to establish a give-and-take, in this case a good compromise is for "he and she" to sit down together and budget the family entertaining on a fair and compatible basis in one of the following ways. One couple may decide to have a few friends over regularly once a week or once a month.

Another couple may prefer dividing "his" and "her" friends into separate hen parties and stag affairs occasionally. Another couple may prefer to go all out and invite everyone they know to a huge bash once a year or so. Some may decide to entertain with another couple or a small group. (See Chapter V)

Whatever the decision, this one social rule always holds fast. No matter how charming, bright, attractive, gay or witty one is, it's not possible to have a successful social life unless hospitality is reciprocated. Now it doesn't necessarily matter if one reciprocates on the same level, tit for tat, but reciprocate one must to the best of one's ability.

Poet-publisher Joseph Addison put it neatly when he wrote in 1702, "For my part I can no more accept a snuffbox without returning my acknowledgements than I can take snuff without sneezing after it."

EFFICIENCY—EFFICIENCY!

The efficient hostess is not always the hardest worker. When asked, "How do you manage to get so much done?" she's apt to reply, "I'm basically really very lazy, I always try to think of the simplest short cuts!"

A useful short-cut for lazy people is to keep a party log or diary similar to the call board used in the theater. (A call board is a meticulously contrived chart showing exactly what should be happening during rehearsals and where).

The real value of a party log lies in recording accurate memos under *post-mortems* for future reference. The queen in "Alice in Wonderland" by Lewis Carroll sums it up rather humorously.

"The horror of that moment," the king went on, "I shall never, *never* forget!"

"You will, though," the queen said, "if you don't make a memorandum of it."

Not only is a party log a time saver in the long run, but it's as much fun to browse through as a photograph album or a first baby-book. It's a snap to make your own by using a looseleaf binder where a page might look like this:

Party for   Where   Date   Time

Dress   Caterer or extra help

Guest list   Yes   No

Menu:

Recipes:

Shopping list:

Food specialties to send for:

Beverages:

Liquor:

Equipment to borrow or rent,
    folding chairs, tables, bars:

Flower arrangement

Table setting

Music

Comments:

House Check List

Is the house number visible—or hidden behind an overgrown bush?

Is the driveway clear—or will Johnny be heartbroken if someone drives over his new tricycle?

Is the car in the garage—or is it taking up good parking space in front of the house?

Are the garage doors closed—or wide open, leaving a hole about as decorative as a missing tooth?

During warm weather are the sprinklers turned off along the sidewalk—presumably everyone has had his shower.

Is the garden hose draped across the walk—or neatly rolled out of the way?

In the winter, is the walk free from snow and the steps clear of ice—or do you carry lots of insurance?

Check List For a Large Party

Table skirt and cloths
Flower decoration, candelabra, candles
Cloth napkins
China
Table Glassware
Flat Silver
Service Silver
Serving trays and platters
Warming stoves, ovens, grills, coffee maker
Matches
Cocktail napkins
Cigarettes, cigars
Candies, Nuts
Parking space
Coat racks and hangers

Bar equipment

Bar table • Linen • Glassware • Bar equipment: bottle openers, mixers, etc. • Wines, Spirits, Mixes, Punches • Garnishes for drinks • Ice cubes, crushed ice, ice molds.

Come for Coffee, Brunch or Lunch

"Heaven is not built of country seats,
but little queer suburban streets."—Christopher Morley

MORNING COFFEE

The morning coffee ritual flowered in the South where entertaining is pleasanter in the cool of the morning than in the heat of the afternoon. Its popularity spread all over the country and especially among young mothers, who like to be home by 3:30 when school lets out. Frequently it precedes a meeting or bridge game, rather than just a leisurely mid-morning pause to visit with friends or neighbors.

In all fairness and with abject apologies to my southern sisters, I must confess that since I'm a "night" person, I avoid morning engagements like a case of ptomaine poisoning. However, it's easy to see the advantage for "day" people, who by

27

9 A.M. have already packed umteen lunches, made the beds, thrown a load of washing into the machine, seen husband and child 1 through 6 off for the day, fed their pets and watered their plants.

For them the house is clean and quiet now and this is the time to invite friends and neighbors in for an old-fashioned Kaffee Klatch or to host a meeting or to entertain out-of-town guests.

KONA COFFEE:

It hardly seems possible that barely three hundred years ago a merchant introduced coffee as a "black soup good for drinking" while today there's hardly a place in the world one can pause without being offered a cup of hospitality.

My favorite coffee took place in Honolulu while visiting my younger sister. (Perhaps the five hour time difference had something to do with this choice because while it's only ten o'clock there it's already three o'clock in the afternoon *my* time and a respectable hour for introductions!)

Anyway at tenish about twenty vivacious girls arrived in bright mumus. Tagging along was the pre-kindergarten crowd for whom my sister had provided an experienced babysitter. The lollipop set were served refreshments (cookies and Kool-aid, what else?) in a designated play area away from the grown-ups (far away from the grown-ups!)

It was easy to "aloha" the guest of honor because I'd been provided with a flower lei of baby orchids. (See directions for making fresh flower lei under decorations, Chapter VIII).

After warm greetings, guests moved to the dining table which was covered with a batik cloth with matching napkins neatly folded beside forks, spoons and a mixed collection of cups and dessert plates. In the center of the table rested a lush arrangement of pineapples, bananas, coconuts and mangos with freshly picked tropical, variegated foliage from the garden. At one of the tables a friend poured that wonderful Island-grown Kona coffee (sold throughout the mainland—in other words, New York to California!) Most coffees are a blend but Kona is not. The secret of its goodness, like French champagne, the great

Bordeaux clarets or Cognac, is climate and location; only in the Kona district can this coffee be produced because the high mountains of Mauna Loa catch the midday clouds and form a natural umbrella over the western slopes.

Kona Coffee Menu

Fresh Pineapple Chunks

Fresh Coconut Bits   Papayas

Kumquat-Macadamia Nut Cake

Coffee

Many popular island dishes are culled from the best of many lands; China, Japan, Korea, the Philippines and, of course, native Hawaiian fare. The latter's contribution and substitute for bread, the staff of life, is poi—but unless one is weaned on it, forget it!

Since our accelerated western influence has touched Hawaii, so often referred to as the crossroads of the world, it's becoming more and more apparent that exciting new combinations of the choicest of east-west dishes are beginning to appear on their exotic tables. For example this Kumquat-Macadamia Nut Cake my sister served for her coffee is an excellent illustration. From China, where the kumquat originated, she borrowed the "golden orange", as it is called there, and from the west she borrowed the Bundt form in which so many famous European coffee cakes are baked.

KUMQUAT-MACADAMIA NUT CAKE

(Served in a 7 1/2 inch bundt form or tube pan)

2 cups flour
2 1/2 teaspoons baking powder
1/4 teaspoon baking soda
1/4 teaspoon salt (omit if nuts are salted)
1/2 cup milk
1/4 cup chopped kumquats
1/4 lb. butter
1 cup sugar
2 large eggs
1/2 cup chopped unsalted Macadamia nuts
3 tablespoons powdered sugar

Set out butter and milk for at least an hour before mixing so that they come to room temperature.

Preheat oven to 350°. In a small mixing bowl, sift together flour (even it it's presifted) baking powder, soda and salt. Drain liquid, chop kumquats fine and add to milk. In a medium-size bowl, cream butter. Add sugar and beat 'til light yellow. Add eggs one at a time and beat until thoroughly blended. Alternate sifted ingredients and milk mixture to creamed mixture, blending together after each addition. Fold in Macadamia nuts. Pour dough into a lightly buttered and floured 1/2-inch bundt form and bake at 350° for one hour. Cool on wire rack and just before serving shake powdered sugar through a fine sieve very lightly, just enough to accentuate the molded pattern of the bundt form. Makes 12 servings.

Addenda: This recipe may be made the day before, also excellent to keep on hand in the freezer. Let the cake cool before freezing or it may turn soggy. Sprinkle with powdered sugar after defrosting.

NO-YEAST BUNDT KUCHEN

I don't know what we'd do without this Bundt Kuchen recipe in our house, because we use it constantly for almost every occasion; morning coffees, (when I can't avoid having one), teas, cocktail suppers and midnight buffets the year 'round. It's especially striking served during the winter season because when the cake is lightly dusted with powdered sugar, the effect reminds one of freshly fallen snow on a rolling countryside. It requires a bundt form. Mine is a heavy old copper one with a crown pattern which I found years ago. But bundt forms are advertised in numerous catalogues (See Sources of Supply).

Most bundt recipes call for yeast, but we've had such good luck with our modified version and so many people have asked for the recipe, here it is! It's one of those cakes that's better on the second and third day, if there's any left.

We set the eggs and butter out of the refrigerator the night before and take the milk out of the refrigerator the first thing in the morning or at least one hour before starting, to make sure everything is at room temperature. This is made in an 8 1/2-inch bundt form.

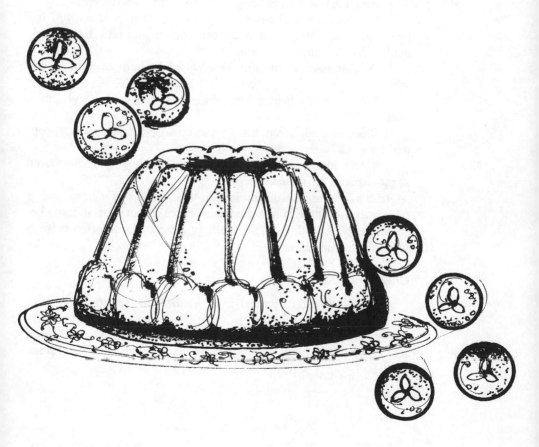

1 cup butter
2 cups sugar
5 egg yolks, slightly beaten
3 cups sifted flour
3 teaspoons baking powder
1 cup milk
5 egg whites, stiffly beaten
1 teaspoon vanilla
1/2 cup raisins
Rind of 1 lemon, grated medium fine
3 tablespoons powdered sugar

1. Cream butter and sugar together in a large mixing bowl until the mixture is light and fluffy. You can use an electric beater or the back of a wooden spoon.

2. Add slightly beaten egg yolks to butter and sugar.

3. Sift flour three times (even presifted flour because you use less flour after sifting). Measure out 3 cups and add 3 teaspoons baking powder and sift again.

4. Add to butter mixture in bowl and alternate with 1 cup milk.

5. Fold in stiffly beaten egg whites, vanilla, raisins and lemon rind.

6. Bake in 350° oven for 45 minutes (With heavy duty copper form allow an extra 20 minutes).

7. Cool; just before serving, sprinkle lightly with powdered sugar. Makes 16 servings.

Addenda: Bundt Kuchen is best made the day before and it freezes beautifully. When freezing let cake cool or it may become soggy. Sprinkle lightly with powdered sugar after defrosting at least two hours.

CLOVE CAKE

A spicy variation of the Bundt Kuchen, also baked in a high tube pan or bundt form; it stays fresh for several days and freezes nicely. Set eggs, butter and milk out of the refrigerator for at least one hour before mixing or until room temperature.

3 cups flour
1 tablespoon powdered cloves

1 tablespoon cinnamon
1/4 teaspoon salt
1/2 lb. butter
2 1/4 cups sugar
5 eggs
1 cup sour or buttermilk
1 teaspoon baking soda

Preheat oven to 350° F. Sift flour twice. The third time sift together with cloves, cinnamon and salt. In a large mixing bowl, cream butter and sugar; add eggs one at a time. Beat well until light and fluffy. Alternate flour mixture with 1/2 cup milk (no soda) adding to creamed butter mixture. Last add 1/2 cup milk mixed with baking soda. Grease and flour tube or bundt form well. Place in oven and bake for 1 hour or until done.

GUAVA JELLY DOUGHNUT

The first Europeans to migrate to Hawaii were the Portuguese, bringing with them not only the ukelele as we know it, but also a most popular delicacy called "selocey", better known to us on the mainland as the doughnut. Here are two new ways of serving it, Hawaiian style.

Cut warm doughnuts in half horizontally and spread with guava jelly—that's all!

Teenagers and their little brothers really love this sweet-tooth Hawaiian concoction! It's one that any young chef can make with ease given half the chance, either at home, at a school picnic or on a summer camp cook-out.

PINEAPPLE-DOUGHNUT SANDWICH

6 plain doughnuts
3 teaspoons butter
2 tablespoons dark brown sugar
1 tablespoon grated orange rind
6 slices canned pineapple rings
6 frilly toothpicks

Preheat oven to 400° F. Cut doughnuts in half horizontally and spread with 1/2 teaspoon butter. Combine sugar and orange rind, sprinkle mixture on half a doughnut. Place slice of canned pineapple between halves and make sandwich. Put in oven for 10 minutes. Remove from oven and insert frilly toothpick in doughnut sandwich and serve warm. Makes 6 servings.

KONA COFFEE COOKIE

> 1 cup butter, (room temperature)
> 1 cup sugar
> 2 eggs
> 1 cup blackstrap molasses
> 1 tablespoon vinegar
> 1 cup hot, very strong coffee
> 1 tablespoon Kahlua liqueur, optional
> 4 1/2 cups sifted flour
> 1 teaspoon ground ginger
> 2 tablespoon soda
> 1 teaspoon salt
> Sliced almonds optional

1. Preheat oven to 375° F. In a medium size bowl, mix butter and sugar, add eggs, molasses, vinegar, coffee and Kahlua (if desired); blend thoroughly.

2. In a large bowl, sift flour, adding ginger, soda and salt. Mix liquid with dry ingredients until smooth.

3. Drop from teaspoon on lightly greased cookie sheet and bake for 10 to 12 minutes.

4. Remove from oven and sprinkle immediately with granulated sugar and place on wire rack to cool.

Optional: After cookies have baked for 5 minutes, place several sliced almonds in center of cookies as petals forming a white ginger flower design.

EGGS VOLCANO

Broadway's Hal Hackady (he and I have collaborated on a play) introduced us to this delightful breakfast dish *a deux;* also tempting after theater or a concert if you enjoy discussing the quality of the performance. It's just as quick to make as French toast.

Hal serves the egg yolks unbroken. However, before eating this dish, the idea is to break the yolks so that they run down over the sides of the meringue making a kind of instant sauce or eggs volcano!

2 slices of raisin bread
2 eggs
Dash of salt
4 slices cheese (Cheddar or American)

1. Preheat oven to 450° F. Toast bread in oven or toaster while you separate the eggs and beat the whites with salt until stiff. (Be careful not to break the yolks because you need them in mint condition later on.)
2. When toast is done place two slices of cheese on each slice of toast and replace in oven until cheese starts to melt.
3. Remove from oven and place a mound of stiffly beaten egg white on each slice of toast. Pile mound as high as you can and then tap slightly with tablespoon to form a slight indentation on the peak. (This is where you'll nest your egg yolk later.)
4. Replace in oven and cook just long enough for the egg white to become firm enough to support the egg yolk. Again remove from oven and place yolks carefully in each depression of the egg white. Replace in oven and cook until yolks are done.

BRUNCHES AND WHAT TO WEAR

The charm of a combination breakfast-lunch is that it's such a genial way to entertain at home! By it's nature, a brunch should be a *gemutlich* affair, and I just can't bring myself to enjoy the formality of dressing for a brunch at a swank hotel for a crowd of fifty people!

It follows then that the setting of a memorable brunch is far more important than the menu. Dining on a shady terrace, a Spanish patio, beside a sparkling pool, under a latticed gazebo— or anywhere in a well-appointed garden—is my number one choice. Dress, of course, should be casual sport clothes.

It's up to the hostess to prepare us for an *al-fresco* setting when she invites us by suggesting what to wear. On the phone, she might say something like this:

"Please come for brunch Sunday to meet our houseguests. We'll be dressed from church, but if it's a nice day, you'll enjoy a dip in the pool, so won't you bring along your suits and towels."

Human beings are, by and large, conformists and dislike appearing singular. Customs vary so from group to group and locale to locale; it's difficult for the most experienced traveler always to be right. In southwest resorts you'll find some tuxedos, but they are mostly worn by the waiters. Here western shirts and levis predominate while in Palm Beach one's best linen cocktail dress can be seen at 10:00 A.M. on Worth Avenue.

Travel agencies make it their business to inform one exactly how little one needs when travelling to faraway places and so do steamship companies. If you're uncertain what to wear do a little advance sleuthing. Most people will be flattered by the question, "What are you wearing to the Smith's on Sunday?" Haven't we all had an unhappy experience in our lives when we wished we'd remembered to ask this simple question. I know I have!

One summer I was invited to a cocktail party for 5 o'clock. I raced home early from the beach on a beautiful, hot summer day, showered, dressed myself in heels and my best linen, drove to the party and noticed through the garden bushes that everyone there was still dressed in beach clothes. Without stopping the car, I returned home, changed into a fresh pair of shorts and blouse and returned to the party, breathless, late, but properly "undressed"!

Elizabeth Hawes, a noted dress designer, believes that the color of a woman's dress must be becoming to her mind, and isn't this particularly true for the hostess? Always wear something you like, that's comfortable, that isn't too loose or too tight or too warm if you wish to remain cool, calm and collected. Take time out during the party to freshen up a bit. A few secret moments by yourself to apply a bit of lipstick or run a comb through your hair will do wonderful things for your nerves. Your serenity will help give the impression all's well—even if there's chaos in the kitchen!

POOLSIDE BRUNCH

Whenever we're invited to an outdoor affair I'm reminded of this amusing story about a woman who planned a garden party and didn't invite her neighbor because she was miffed with her. At the last minute she relented and telephoned to invite her neighbor who without hesitation replied, "It's too late—I've already prayed for rain!"

Well, we had prayed for sunshine and fortunately on the day of the brunch everything appeared in readiness around the pool. We were offered the choice of a Bloody Mary or Bullshot or a non-alcoholic Red Orange Juice, each mixed ahead ready to be poured over ice. (Both Bloody Marys and Bullshots are made with vodka, a drink that has rapidly overtaken gin in popularity in the United States.)

It's wise not to serve drinks in breakable glasses around a pool—too many bare feet. Invento puts out a sturdy, clear, very thin plastic container that is disposable or can be washed and used over and over again, and won't break if dropped. You can order them imprinted with any personal design you fancy; with your name, crest, poolhouse or whatever. (See Sources of Supply.)

Sunday Chef Poolside Brunch

Bloody Mary (see Chapter IV)   Bullshot
Red Orange Juice (Mix an equal
part of cranberry and orange juice,
sweeten to taste and serve chilled).
Crackers and Tortilla Chips
Omelet with Herbs, Chives, Cheese,
Bacon, Onions, Red Caviar or Jam
Hard Rolls   Sweet Butter
Tea or Coffee

OMELETS WITH A FLAIR

Sunday chefs who delight in demonstrating their culinary skills might do well to take a tip from Chef Rudolph Stanish, caterer and professional omelet-maker extraordinaire. He combines a bit of legerdemain with his culinary ability—or why else is he flown from one end of the country to the other, preparing from twenty to thirty thousand omelets a year for leading figures of the theater including playwright Edward Albee and Mrs. Richard Rodgers, along with socialites, Mrs. Paul Mellon, Mrs. John Hay Whitney, and Mrs. Alfred Gwynne Vanderbilt.

Stanish—everyone calls him Rudi—turns out omelets not only for wedding breakfasts and hunt breakfasts, but for Christmas Eve gatherings, New Year's Eve parties, after-theater parties and just about any happy occasion. Manhattan-based, Rudi is also food consultant to such well-known clients as Restaurant Associates who operate LaFonda del Sol, the Four Seasons and the Forum of the Twelve Caesars.

I watched Rudi perform his magic against a backdrop of blue delphinium at an outdoor wedding breakfast. Bringing his own equipment, including a portable propane-fueled Bernz-O-Matic burner and several 10″ aluminum omelet pans (See Sources of Supply) he deftly set up his equipment on two long tables covered with white cloths. On the tables he placed numerous small bowls filled with a choice of chopped herbs, chives, parsley, onions, grated cheddar cheese, bits of bacon, red caviar, sour cream, apricot jam and powdered sugar.

It doesn't take long before the orders come hot and fast! "Make mine cheese" or "I'll try the caviar and sour cream" or "One apricot jam and powdered sugar" and to our astonishment, Rudi, the Omelet Man, delivers in seconds—thirty seconds to an omelet to be exact!

Here's Rudolph Stanish's own omelet recipe for 25. He tells me the secret is in the water!

BASIC OMELET

    1 cup cold water
    1 tablespoon salt
    1 teaspoon Tabasco sauce
    5 dozen fresh eggs, room temperature
    3/4 lb. butter

1. In a small bowl mix water, salt and Tabasco.
2. Break eggs into very large bowl (5- or 6-quart capacity) and beat until well blended with an egg beater.
3. Add salt-water and Tabasco mixture to beaten eggs and stir well. Set aside until ready to use.
4. Heat individual omelet pan to medium and melt one tablespoon butter until it bubbles.
5. Select any one or combination of several ingredients now i.e., chopped herbs, parsley, chives, crumbled bacon, finely chopped onion or mild grated cheddar cheese and put in pan.
6. Add a dipper of 3/4 cup egg liquid and stir with a fork flat on the pan making one fast circular motion. This movement will distribute the herbs or bacon etc. evenly throughout the omelet. While making the circular motion, shake the pan to and fro until the eggs congeal and the bottom of the pan is covered with egg. Roll onto heated plate and garnish with parsley. Serves 25.

Addenda : *Always* use salted butter. Keep pan on a medium flame with the heat readily adjustable. Have ingredients and things to be added within reach. Banish everything but the care of the omelet from your mind and concentrate on the eggs. Serve immediately. Make only one omelet at a time.

RED CAVIAR OMELET FOR ONE

Before risking inviting two dozen neighbors, you might like to try an omelet with red caviar and sour cream for yourself.

1 tablespoon water
1/4 teaspoon salt (scant)
Dash of Tabasco sauce
3 eggs
1 tablespoon salted butter
1 tablespoon red caviar
2 tablespoons sour cream
1 tablespoon chopped parsley

1. Mix water, salt and parsley in a cup.
2. Break eggs into small bowl, beat slightly.
3. Add salt-water mixture to beaten eggs and stir well. Set aside until ready to use.
4. Heat omelet pan to medium and melt one tablespoon butter until it bubbles.

5. Pour egg mixture into pan and stir with a fork flat on the pan making one fast circular motion. Shake the pan to and fro until eggs congeal and the bottom of the pan is covered with egg. Roll onto heated plate.

6. Make an incision lengthwise (about 3 inches long) and spread it apart and neatly spoon in the mixture of red caviar and sour cream. Sprinkle with parsley and eat hot.

CHAMPAGNE BRUNCH

For those darling people who do not choose to be "center stage" flipping omelets and who much prefer preparing things as far ahead as possible, this menu should suit just fine! Practically all that needs doing on the day is to pop the cork for the champagne, that is if you set the table the night before.

Champagne Brunch Menu

Champagne Sec
Sherried Sweetbreads and Mushrooms Rolled in Crepes
Mini-marmalade Sandwich   Bibb Lettuce Salad
Fresh Berries and Fruits
Coffee

SHERRIED SWEETBREADS

Sherried Sweetbreads and mushrooms rolled in crepes may be done in three simple stages. The crepes can be made weeks ahead and frozen (See crepe recipe Chapter VI). The day before the brunch cook the sweetbreads, sauté the mushrooms and combine with sauce. On the morning of the brunch spread sweet-bread mixture over defrosted crepes, roll and warm in oven until ready to serve.

    2 pounds sweetbreads
    1 teaspoon salt
    1 tablespoon vinegar
    1 pound fresh mushrooms
    4 tablespoon butter

Soak sweetbreads in cold water 20 minutes. Drain. Cook twenty minutes in a quart of boiling salt water with vinegar. Drain water and plunge sweetbreads into cold water. Chill in refrigerator. Remove pipes and membranes; cut or break sweet-breads into small pieces. Slice off the end of mushroom stems and rinse under a light stream of cold water and drain. Slice mushrooms. In a heavy medium-size skillet heat butter then add mushrooms. Turn with a pancake turner as edges begin to brown slightly and mushrooms turn golden. About 5 minutes. Combine sweetbreads and mushrooms.

Sauce

    3 tablespoons butter
    3 tablespoons flour
    1 chicken boullion cube
    1 cup hot water
    1/2 cup cream
    Dash of salt
    Dash of paprika
    3 tablespoons Sherry wine

Melt butter in saucepan and add flour. Stir. Place chicken boullion cube in cup of hot water until dissolved and add to heated mixture while stirring. Add cream. Bring to boil while still stirring. Add seasoning and Sherry. Combine sweetbreads, mushrooms and sauce and refrigerate until ready to serve. Save a little sauce to pour over the finished crepes. Defrost the crepes. Preheat oven 275° and spread sweetbread and mushroom mix-ture over crepes. Roll and place in an oblong baking dish ready for serving and cover with remaining sauce. Warm in oven at 275° for 20 to 25 minutes. Makes enough for 12 crepes or 6 servings.

MINI-MARMALADE SANDWICH

Remove the crust from thin slices of white bread. Spread with soft butter and orange marmalade. Put two slices together. Melt a tablespoon of butter in frying pan and fry slowly on both sides until golden. Cut diagonally twice into quarters before serving.

Addenda: You can prepare this one hour ahead and keep it toasty in a warm oven. The butter keeps bread from drying out.

FARCIES A LA PRINCESSE

How many women can you name who are young, beautiful, talented, and titled, live in a royal palace with a prince and have three lovely children? Of course, there's only one, Her Serene Highness, Princess Grace of Monaco.

Philadelphia-born Princess Grace often serves *Farcies,* one of her favorite recipes, by the pool for lunch. Farcies are stuffed vegetables which can be served hot or cold along with a large tossed green salad. Here is the Princess's own recipe for this delicacy.

You may fill either tomatoes, eggplant or zucchini or a combination of all three with the following ingredients, but this quantity is sufficient for 8 large tomatoes. There are no hard and fast rules to the recipe, and every local housewife has her own way of making them. Some prefer, for instance, to use rice in place of the potato; others also add a bit of raw spinach. The overall characteristic of Farcies is that they are usually peppery and well flavored with garlic.

> 8 large tomatoes
> 1 medium-size boiled onion
> 3/4 lb. boiled ham
> 1 crushed clove garlic
> 2 tablespoons mashed potatoes or rice
> 1/4 cup finely chopped parsley
> 3/4 cup finely grated Italian Parmesan cheese
> 1 large beaten egg
> Large dash of freshly ground pepper
> Salt
> 3/4 cup breadcrumbs

Preheat oven to 400° F. Cut deep narrow hole in firm large tomatoes. Scoop out inside and save. In your blender mix boiled
onion, ham, garlic, cheese, potato, parsley, seasoning and tomato
pulp at medium speed for 15 seconds. Remove from blender and
bind together with beaten egg. Fill tomatoes with mixture. Top
with dry breadcrumbs and bake in oven for 15 minutes. Makes 8
   Addenda: To replace the tomato cases with eggplant or
zucchini, cook the vegetable whole in boiling salted water with
a slice of onion added for flavor. When tender but still firm,
drain and cut in half. Blend the ingredients for the filling as
given above, stuff and bake as directed.

AN INVITATION TO LUNCH

Giving a luncheon is a joy—to be as free and creative as one
likes—and there's usually a marvelous reason for celebrating! A
bridal shower, baby shower, farewell or welcome-home, birthday, victory at the club competition or graduation are all dreamy
occasions for a luncheon.
   When there's a ready-made theme, party planning is a breeze
for the hostess with a flair who steals a few tricks from the
theater where entertainment is "king" Her invitations announce
coming events like the theater lights on a marquee.
   An invitation may be as informal as a personal post card or
engraved on white vellum; it may be a jingle of your own or a
champagne glass mailed in a box of pop corn that's marked
"to be filled at---"; it can be as sentimental as a locket or as
corny as a bandana! (Both from the dime store.)
   As far back as 1847, Lady Goon was plagued with the desire
to mail an original and unusual invitation. She went to a great
deal of trouble and arranged for the printing of a special issue
stamp showing the profile of a lovely lady somewhat resembling
Victoria. One of these unused Mauritius stamps sold many years
later for over $20,000 in London.
   One can't help but speculate why all the stamps were not used
for mailing her invitations? Did Lady Goon black pencil a name
on her list in anger—or with regret? Or had she, with foresight,
ordered extra stamps? We'll never know.
   But the urge to be original still persists for I've noticed invitations that have come through the mail with special com-

memorative stamps that jibe with the party theme. For instance, a yacht club sent invitations for their closing gala ball using the commemorative stamp of a painting by Thomas Eakins, "The Biglin Brothers Racing." What a subtle touch!

Sometimes it's not easy to find just the kind of printed invitation one is looking for on the market. Then it's fun to improvise. This is what I had to do when I looked for a "Bon Voyage" invitation. I found some informals with a pale green marine scene across which I scrawled "Bon Voyage!" in green ink. Inside on one page I put the date, time and place; on the other page I wrote "Please bring an intangible gift—a travel tip, a hint, a suggestion or a word picture of a memory, a scent, a sound or image; a toast."

BON VOYAGE LUNCHEON:

All the guests arrived with amusing anecdotes of experiences and memories of their travels, some in poem, song or rhyme, with loads of advice for our peripatetic friend as to where and where not to eat, shop and stay.

After cocktails and during the meal these poems were read, memories kindled, toasts toasted and information shared with the prospective traveller who also happened to be an avid amateur painter. Intermittently, fake telegrams were delivered* that sent everyone into gales of laughter. Here are a few samples.

There's no question when guests are involved it's bound to help make things go! To this day Caroline cherishes her Bon Voyage scrapbook and the memory of a very personal, hearty send-off.

*This wasn't hard to do because who remembers what a Western Union boy looks like?

ASK FOR MARCEL AT THE LOUVRE AND SAY I SENT YOU

CHARLIE BROWN

DON'T DRINK THE WATER JUST THE WINE--
OR YOU'LL BE SORRY CAROLINE

THE AMERICAN MEDICAL SOCIETY

APPOINTMENT SET TO SKETCH PRINCESS GRACE OF MONACO
FOR THE COVER OF TIME

THE EDITORS

Bon Voyage Luncheon Menu

Cocktails   Hot Cheese Cookies*
        Shrimp and Artichoke Casserole
Chilled Mandarin Oranges   Rice with Parsley
                Rolls
Coffee   Mocha Marshmallow Mousse

*Hot Cheese Cookie recipe under hors d'oeuvre in Chapter IV.

SHRIMP AND ARTICHOKE CASSEROLE

This Shrimp and Artichoke Casserole recipe with an international flavor came from the family kitchen records of Adlai Stevenson's mother. When Stevenson was U.S. Minister, Chief of U.S. Delegation for the United Nations, he served this dish to President Kennedy and U.N. Acting Secretary General U Thant. Even though Stevenson had eaten the same dish the day before, he enjoyed it so much that he asked the chef to prepare it again on the following day when lunching with the President.

  1 lb. shrimp in shell, fresh or frozen
  2 tablespoons salt
  1/4 lb. fresh or canned mushrooms
    sliced medium
  2 tablespoons butter
  1 1/2 cup cream sauce
  3 tablespoons butter
  3 tablespoons flour
  1 1/2 cup milk
  Salt and pepper to taste
  1 can (20 oz.) artichoke hearts
  1/4 cup dry sherry wine
  1 tablespoon Worcestershire sauce
  1/4 cup grated Parmesan Cheese
  1 teaspoon paprika

  1. Plunge washed frozen shrimp in 1 1/2 quarts of boiling salted water and let boil 10 to 14 minutes or until tender. (Fresh shrimp take less than 5 minutes.) Let shrimps cool in liquid. Drain and remove shell and black vein.
  2. Slice mushrooms and sauté in butter in a small skillet at medium temperature until golden.
  3. Make cream sauce: In a double boiler heat 3 tablespoons butter, 3 tablespoons flour, 1 1/2 cup milk, salt and pepper. Beat with egg beater to prevent lumps from forming. Cook for about 5 minutes.
  4. Drain water from artichoke hearts and arrange hearts in a buttered 2 quart baking dish. Spread shrimp and sautéed mushrooms over artichokes.

5. Add sherry to cream sauce, stir and add Worcestershire sauce and stir again. Pour cream sauce over shrimp and artichokes. Sprinkle top generously with Parmesan cheese and paprika. Bake for 30 to 40 minutes in 375° oven and serve hot. Makes 6 servings.

MOCHA MARSHMALLOW MOUSSE

It's so much easier and very nice too, to serve an individual dessert, especially for a luncheon. And the easiest dessert ever is this Mocha Marshmallow Mousse. A little portion goes a long way because it's quite rich. I served it in individual small stemmed sherbet glasses on a plate with a paper doily and two lady fingers on each plate. In every serving I inserted a miniature paper flag. (A packaged assortment of flags is available in your local dime store or your stationery store.) The sherbet glasses were carried in on a tray and the various flags of all nations grouped together made a gay bon-voyage bouquet.

      30 marshmallows
      1 cup strong coffee
      1 cup whipping cream
      1/2 teaspoon vanilla
      or 2 tablespoons Kahlua

1. Cut up marshmallows and dissolve in hot coffee in double boiler and cool.
2. Whip cream and fold into mixture. Add vanilla or Kahlua.
3. Pour into sherbet glasses and set in refrigerator. Makes 6 servings.

INTERNATIONAL SMORGASBORD:

Give travellers a rousing send-off by serving a native product from each country on their itinerary. On a large platter arrange a mixture of cold cuts and place a matching flag of the land on the *Swiss* Cheese, *Danish* Ham, *Portuguese* Sardines, *Italian* Salami, *Greek* Olives, *Russian* Rye Bread, served with *German* Beer or *French* Wine.

One can enjoy an international Smorgasbord at any time—for luncheon, dinner or an evening snack (see Sources of Supply for party props).

A LUNCHEON SYMPHONY MENU

Once in awhile there's an occasion when a "little" luncheon at home for both men and women is a pleasant diversion. I attended such a gathering in honor of a visiting conductor and his wife, Monsieur and Madame Paul Paray, where the theme for the décor was musical, of course. Our imaginative hostess used sheet music for table-mats, and a violin and a bow set among potted violets as the centerpiece on a base of records—a nice low arrangement to help span lively discussion.

Naturally the stereo was turned on softly playing some of Monsieur Paray's recordings while we were lunching.

Luncheon Symphony Menu

Chicken Boullion
Crabmeat on Rusk
Celery   Olives, Green Pickles, Relish
Vanilla Ice Cream
with
Crême de Menthe Sauce
or Maraschino Cherry Sauce
Tea

CRABMEAT (OR TUNA) ON RUSK

2 packages (3 oz. each) cream cheese
1/8 lb. butter
1 tablespoon lemon juice
1 teaspoon Worcestershire sauce
1 tablespoon minced onion
1 (7 oz.) can crab meat or tuna
1 package Holland Rusk
2 large tomatoes in 6 slices
6 slices Old English cheese
3 strips partially cooked bacon

Preheat oven to 450° F.

1. Cream the cream cheese with butter, lemon juice, Worcestershire sauce, minced onion in a medium size bowl.

2. In a separate bowl flake crab meat and remove bones. (If tuna fish is used instead, drain tuna.) Add to cream cheese, and mix together.

3. Divide mix and shape into six patties. Put each on a piece of Holland Rusk. On top place a slice of tomato, a slice of Old English cheese, and half a strip of partially cooked bacon.

4. Bake 10 minutes in 450° oven and 10 more minutes under broiler or until cheese melts and bacon is crisp. Makes 6 patties. *Addenda*: Crabmeat on Rusk is very popular with men so be prepared to serve seconds!

MARASCHINO CHERRY SAUCE

    2 tablespoons cornstarch
    1/3 cup sugar
    2/3 cup water
    1/2 cup maraschino cherry juice
    1/4 cup maraschino cherries
    1/2 tablespoon butter

Mix the cornstarch and sugar in a saucepan. Add water and cherry juice and boil for 2 minutes. Add cherries and butter. Let cool. Makes scant 2 cups.

SUB-TEEN BIRTHDAY LUNCHEON

Every "little Miss" adores to dress up for a luncheon preceeding a Saturday matinee or swimming party.

Our doorbell begins ringing promptly on the appointed hour. As soon as the youngsters finish "ohing" and "ahing" over the presents, the group moves on to the dining room, where a pink and white table is set.

My all-time favorite centerpiece for this celebration is composed of an ordinary small leafless branch with numerous twigs that's been sprayed a shocking pink and placed securely in a deep flower pot filled with sand. (The branch can be anchored to a pinholder.) An ice cream cone is tied on to each twig with a pink ribbon. Nestled in the ice cream cone is a bright pink carnation corsage—a souvenir for every young lady present.

Carnation Birthday Luncheon

Turkey Salad
Tomato Wedges   Olives   Hard-cooked Eggs
Garnished with Bouquet of Watercress
Hot Biscuits or Scones (see recipe in Chapter III)
Iced Chocolate Float
Vanilla Cookies

TURKEY SALAD A LA WOMAN'S EXCHANGE

There still are a number of people who sigh over the wonderful chicken salad served by the Woman's Exchange in Detroit, and although the famous dining and catering spot of the socially prominent is no longer in existence, the recipe for this popular dish fortunately is a matter of public record. The secret is deceptively simple, because almost as important as what was put in the salad is what was left out!

No onions or celery are added to the water in which the chickens are cooked; no fancy spices, capers or seasonings are added to the dressing; and no peas, marshmallows or hardboiled eggs are included to stretch the salad or dull the honest-to-goodness chicken flavor.

No indeed! The hens are always cooked whole and simmered slowly in just enough water to keep the broth rich and delicious. They are cooled slowly with the skin intact to keep the meat moist and placed in the refrigerator until ready to be cut up for salad.

If there is a secret, it's the dressing—a combination of two recipes mixed together—one-half mayonnaise and one-half boiled dressing, both recipes originated by cooks named Betty. But please don't use the dressings separately—they're meant to go together.

Now instead of boiling several hens, which is what one would have to do for a group of 16 people, I've found it much simpler and just as delicious to cook a small turkey or cacklebird, either fresh or frozen. Here is my own version of this juicy, tender and tasty salad.

For a Saturday luncheon for 16 girls, I buy an eleven lb. turkey, preferably fresh. If a fresh turkey is not available, get a frozen turkey on Thursday and let it defrost at room temperature overnight. Be sure to remove the giblets from the inside after thawing.

On Friday morning, place the turkey in a 12-quart kettle, adding 4 quarts of cold water and turn on medium high flame. When water boils, reduce to low and let simmer for 5 hours covered. Drain liquid into bowl, cool and keep refrigerated. (When thoroughly chilled, separate white layer of fat from jellied soup stock. This fat is wonderful for making hashed or fried potatoes, it can be frozen too. The soup stock may be mixed in a blender with leftover vegetables such as lima beans, carrots, broccoli etc. and a little water and seasoning, or combined with sauces.)

The salad dressing may be made Friday or several days ahead and kept in refrigerator.

Mixed Dressing: Mayonnaise Half

    3 egg yolks
    2 teaspoons vinegar
    1 2/3 cups salad oil
    3/4 teaspoon salt
    1/4 teaspoon dry mustard
    Few grains white pepper

Chill egg yolk, vinegar, oil. In a medium bowl mix salt, mustard and pepper. Add egg yolks and blend. Add 1 teaspoon vinegar and mix well. Add teaspoon salad oil at a time, beating with a rotary beater until 1/4 cup has been used. Then add remaining oil in increasing amount alternating the last 1/3 cup with remaining vinegar. (For blender, put egg yolks, vinegar, and seasonings in jar, turn on blender and slowly pour oil; blend until thick.) Makes 1 pint.

Cooked Dressing Half

    4 teaspoons sugar
    2 teaspoons salt
    1/8 teaspoon mustard
    2/3 cup flour (sifted before measured)
    2/3 cup vinegar
    1 cup water
    4 egg yolks
    1/8 teaspoon Worcestershire sauce

In top of double boiler combine sugar, salt, mustard, flour. Place on bottom of boiler. Stir in vinegar and water slowly, beat with egg beater to prevent lumps and cook until thick and there is no starchy taste. Remove from heat and add beaten egg yolks and Worcestershire sauce. Mix. Makes 1 pint.

Assembly of Turkey Salad

On Saturday, cut up white and dark meat of turkey in nice-sized even chunks. Add 1 cup small-diced celery and mix one cup mayonnaise with 1 cup cooked dressing for an eleven-pound turkey.

Serve on individual plates garnished with parsley, olives, wedges of tomatoes and hard boiled eggs. Makes 16 servings.

ICED CHOCOLATE FLOAT

> Chocolate syrup
> Ice Cubes
> Whipped Cream
> Root Beer or Coffee
> Chocolate Ice Cream

Put two tablespoons of chocolate syrup and an ice cube into a tall glass. Fill with root beer or lukewarm coffee and a ball of chocolate ice cream. Top with a teaspoon of whipped cream. Garnish with carnation petals.

DESSERT LUNCHEON

For the last ten years my investment club has met once a month at 1:30 for dessert luncheon. During these years we've eaten our way through chocolate brownies, pecan rolls, lemon rolls, meringues and every kind of coffee ring known to Betty Crocker, both homemade and store bought.

We've used each other as guinea pigs for prize recipes culled from newspapers, magazines and even chain letters. Sometimes there's been too much and other times not enough. Sometimes the dessert has been a gooey disappointment and other times it's been heaven! At our next meeting, this well-tested dessert will be served:

PEANUT BRITTLE SURPRISE

1 3/4 cup sifted flour
2 teaspoons baking powder
1/2 teaspoon salt
1/3 cup butter
1 cup sugar
2 eggs, beaten
1/2 cup milk
1/2 teaspoon vanilla

Preheat oven to 350° F.

Sift together flour, baking powder and salt. In a separate medium size bowl, cream butter, add sugar gradually and beat until light and fluffy. In a third small bowl beat eggs well, add to butter mixture. Add sifted ingredients alternately with milk and vanilla to butter mixture, stirring after each addition until batter is smooth. Spread quite thin in oblong 8" x 12" or 9" x 13" pan. Bake in moderate oven 350°F for 20 to 25 minutes. Cut into 12 squares for individual portions, slice horizontally and spread topping between and around sides of cake.

Topping:

1/4 pound butter
2 cups powdered sugar
4 egg yolks
1 pint whipping cream
1/2 teaspoon vanilla
Several pieces crushed peanut brittle

In a medium size mixing bowl, cream butter. Add sugar gradually and beat until light and fluffy. Add egg yolks and beat well. Whip cream, add vanilla and fold into butter mixture, spread thick over cake and sprinkle with crushed peanut brittle. (To crush peanut brittle, place between folds of a dish towel and crush with a mallet or hammer.) Makes 12 servings.

Addenda: You can substitute a yellow cake mix or a ready-made angel-food cake and merely use the icing sprinkled with peanut brittle. Caution: Serve at room temperature for easy cutting and best flavor.

TRICK AND TREAT

Once in awhile it's nice to have a trick up one's sleeve that can be prepared on the spur of the moment; a quick, easy dessert for unexpected company; something that doesn't need to be baked because we already may have a casserole or roast in the oven; something that doesn't need to sit in the refrigerator overnight; something that tastes so divine, your guests will swear you've spent the day in the kitchen! And unless your cupboard is bare, chances are you might not even need to go marketing—if you're one who likes to improvise.

This recipe is not new, it was old in Martha Washington's day and I'm sure she cherished it as much as I do today.

What's it called?

It's called "Trifle" a puzzling name but one of the dictionary definitions for the word is *trickery* which explains a lot, because it's merely a combination of leftover cake, custard, jelly, fruit, liquor and topped with whipped cream if you like and sprinkled with nuts if you have some.

This is the way we like it best, but I'll give you the substitutions just for fun too.

TRIFLE

Custard

> 2 cups milk or cream
> 3 tablespoons granulated sugar
> 4 egg yolks
> 2 teaspoons vanilla or vanilla pudding; (use 2
>   packages if you omit whipped cream)

Cake

> 3 dozen ladyfingers or cookies, macaroons, leftover
>   yellow or gold cake or any combination you have.

Jelly

> 1/2 cup red currant jelly or apple jelly or whatever
>   you fancy.

Fruit

> 1 cup applesauce or bananas or fresh berries

Liquor

> 1 jigger Cointreau or brandy, Tiddy's, sherry or white
>   wine

Topping

    1 1/2 cups whipped cream or whipped topping or
            extra portion of vanilla pudding

Nuts

    2/3 cup toasted, slivered almonds or chopped pecans,
            Macadamia nuts or walnuts

In the top of a medium-size double boiler, heat cream and sugar. In a medium-size mixing bowl beat egg yolks then add them to the liquid on top of double boiler stirring until it forms a thick sauce in about 3 or 4 minutes. Let cool. Add vanilla and stir.

Spread ladyfingers on bottom and sides of a glass or china serving bowl and sprinkle with Cointreau until the liquor is absorbed by the cake.

Top the ladyfingers with jelly and applesauce, cover with some custard, add another layer of ladyfingers and repeat alternating with Cointreau, jelly, applesauce, custard. Put in refrigerator to chill until ready to serve. If you like, top with whipped cream and nuts.

Note: One package vanilla pudding mix may be substituted for homemade custard.

SURPRISE BOX LUNCH

A variation of our usual Dessert Luncheon is to have each person bring a box lunch for one. After everyone has arrived, the boxes are exchanged with the person to the left. (No favoritism, please!) The hostess serves coffee and cake.

Many of the girls enjoy decorating the boxes as artistically on the outside as they do the goodies on the inside and one of the perkiest box lunches I ever saw was wrapped simply in red and white striped sailcloth (a paper design) and tied with matching red, rick-rack.

Surprise Box Lunch

Meatloaf on French Bread
Chinese Hard-cooked Egg (Chapter IV)
Ring of Green Pepper, Carrot
and Celery Sticks
Midget Pickled Corn on the Cob (Sold whole in glass jars)
Black Olives

CREAMY MEATLOAF

2 pounds ground round steak
2 eggs
2 slices whole wheat bread
1 pound cottage cheese
1 cup yogurt
1 teaspoon monosodium glutamate
1 package Lipton dehydrated onion soup
Dash of Beau Monde seasoning (Spice Islands)
1/2 cup catsup

1. Preheat oven to 250°F. Mix everything except the catsup together in a large bowl and let stand for half an hour. Shape into loaf.
2. Put in an 8" x 12" pan and bake uncovered for two hours
3. The last 1/2 hour, cover with catsup. Serve cold or hot. Makes 10 servings.

BOX LUNCHES AND SUPPERS

Box lunches or suppers are popular for five or five hundred and are ideal for business meetings; club meetings, garden parties, picnics, outings on chartered bus trips for theater parties, football games, etc. It's fun to decorate the containers for men with a gay bow-tie or boutonniere and the ladies' box lunch or basket with a fluffy bow or corsage. When serving chicken, it's also a good way to distinguish dark meat from white meat.

For elegant "cotillion" suppers, where the menu might include such fancies as Rock Lobster tail which has been removed from the shell then replaced and garnished, served with ravigote sauce—for such a special occasion one can line a basket with a linen napkin or roll the silverware in a linen napkin topped with a corsage, and enclose a split bottle of wine.

Menu for Box Lunch or Supper:

Choice of baked ham, corned beef, roast beef, cold steak or
     sliced chicken sandwich.
     Hard-boiled egg, or olives
     Mandarin orange or banana
Choice of container with potato salad, cole slaw, cottage cheese
     and chives, potato chips
Choice of brownies, doughnuts, French pastry, peppermints

Beverages:

Serve a mug of hot soup first (recipe below). With lunch or supper serve hot or iced coffee or tea, depending on the climate; or soft drinks, beer or wine.

SOUP STOCK

Some people love to gnaw the rib bones of roast beef privately, but I prefer to use them as soup stock.

Barely cover leftover roast beef bones (or turkey or chicken bones and scraps) with cold water. Add an onion, cut up piece of celery with leaves, a chopped carrot, a few sprigs of chopped parsley, one tomato (raw or stewed). Bring to a boil then reduce heat to simmer and cook for 2 hours. Remove from stove and strain through colander into mixing bowl and let cool. Place in refrigerator several hours or until fat forms solid crust. Skim fat from top. This stock is delicious when put in blender with leftover cooked vegetables such as peas, carrots, spinach, broccoli, lima beans, cauliflower, etc. Use 1 cup chicken stock to 1 cup milk for creamed soups.

Tea for 2 or 102

*"There are few hours in life more agreeable
than the hour dedicated to the ceremony known
as afternoon tea."—Henry James*

What magic turns the simple act of serving a cup of tea into a bewitching ceremony?

The secret may well depend on the conspicuous consumption of goods as Thorstein Veblen puts it to us in his *Theory of the Leisure Class,* or—the more paraphernalia the better! For instance, drop in to the world-renowned hotel in Hamburg, Germany, the Vier Jahreszeiten, where the trim waiter will bring, along with your tea, an assortment of fifteen utensils (I've counted them); a cup, saucer, plate, teapot, pot of hot water, pitcher of cream or milk, sugar, both cubed and granulated, wedges of lemon with a lemon squeezer on a plate, silver tea strainer, plus silverware. All this is presented on a fresh white tablecloth with white linen napkins and a nosegay of fresh flowers.

The tea ceremony in Japan is even more precise; hot tea is served in delicate porcelain bowls to guests seated on cushions on the floor of a specially designed teahouse; in the Near

Each one is served hot tea in a glass; in England tea is brewed and served in an antique china cup in front of a small glowing fire; wherever tea is served one delights in this lovely ceremony when it is staged correctly.

But too many teas in our own country, I'm afraid, are not staged correctly. Often they're stiff affairs where a large assortment of gooey pink and green cream cheese sandwiches are consumed in a hushed atmosphere. And why, oh why should this be, when the real reason for a tea is always an auspicious, happy occasion, such as moving into a new home; announcing an engagement or honoring a bride or a debutante; saluting a new college president or any V.I.P.; thanking volunteers for a job well done, entertaining sorority sisters, dedicating a building or welcoming friends and family.

Let's run through a fresh bouquet of ideas starting with an elegant small tea, a Devonshire tea, an Easter Sunday tea, a strudel tea, and winding up with a very gay champagne tea!

How can we create a gay, spirited mood that the stylish tea-time custom deserves? One way is to pamper our guests with tender loving care from the very moment he approaches the house. I like to decorate the front door or entrance not only during the Christmas season but for any kind of a party at home or at a club with just a small accent that carries out the party theme and sings out a warm welcome. In the summer it may be no more than an arrangement of potted geraniums on the stoop, whereas for a bridal party we once used white paper doves nestled on the door knocker, and on Easter Sunday we made a wreath using wire coat hangers trimmed with real carrots, and in the middle of this bounty sat what appeared to be a very contented stuffed rabbit.

Have someone stationed inside the door to greet guests with a pleasant "hello" and help them with their hats and coats or I like the whimsical idea of hanging a fancy bonnet over the bedroom door to help guide the way to this improvised coat room.

Be sure to designate a bathroom for your guests and alert the family to be especially careful to leave it as polished and bright as they find it. Convenient fingertip guest towels are available in either disposable paper, linen or terry cloth in attractive colors and designs or monograms. Keep a bottle of air freshener handy, check on the supply of toilet tissue and place a few additional conveniences within easy reach such as safety pins, aspirin, etc. A tiny fresh flower arrangement or just a single perfect bloom next to the mirror is a cheerful touch.

After removing jackets or coats, our guests move into the living room where they will first greet the hostess and chat with people they know, be introduced to newcomers, or in a large group they will take the initiative and introduce themselves, for the roof, as they say, serves as an introduction. If the tea is given in honor of someone, the hostess should see to it that all the guests are introduced to the honored guest and at a large party it's a good idea for her to ask close friends to help make these introductions.

THIS BUSINESS OF INTRODUCTION

How many times have we heard someone say, "Oh, she's stuck up! I've been introduced to her twice and she doesn't remember me!"

Listen with relief to what the New York Society of Self-Culture had to say in 1904.

"An introduction may be cordially recognized ten years after it has taken place or it may be worth nothing after two hours . . . It's not necessary to bow and strive to recall the names of all those persons to whom one has been hurriedly and informally introduced at a large reception . . . unless the meeting proves to be agreeable and conversation ensues."

And what to do with that forever coy, foolishly irritating soul who saunters up to us and says, "I'll bet you don't remember me, do you?" Three cheers to the courageous fellow who replied, "Lady, you win that bet!"

How grateful we are to that special someone who kindly says, "My name is George Smith. We met at the Wilson's last month. It's nice to see you again!"

Emily Post condones only one category of information to be conveyed during an introduction, that of family relationship but I've often wished I could assign name tags with a few pertinent remarks describing the idiosyncrasies of each guest. One might print, "Don't ask her about her health—she'll tell you!" or "Talk about anything except taxes!" or "This one likes to pinch!"

Unfortunately the day will never come when we can use these name tags, but we *can* brief our guests when we're entertaining a prominent personality.

At a posh party recently, a friend of mine struck up a very pleasant conversation with another guest—he didn't catch the name—

> "It's been so enjoyable talking to you, where are you from?"
> "I'm from Norway," the guest replied.
> "How interesting. And what do you do there?"
> "I'm the king," was the simple reply.

AN INFORMAL TEA

One of the most charming continental hostesses I know does much of her informal entertaining with "little teas", so much so in fact, that she even had a large revolving low coffee table made-to-order, a kind of king-size, Lazy-Susan, and on this she places assorted finger sandwiches, cookies and cakes that taste as good as they look. In the summer she moves this table onto a screened porch off the garden and serves iced tea in tall glasses with a sprig of fresh mint. It's a treat to visit with this jolly lady and to meet the medley of interesting people she always seems to attract.

I've always yearned for just such a lovely revolving table, but unfortunately most of us have to make do with what we have— either a stationary coffee table, TV snack tables, a tea cart or a bridge table covered with a pretty cloth. On this we set a tray with our tea things and while pouring from our china or silver teapot, we inquire, "Lemon, cream or milk? Saccharine or sugar? How many lumps, please?" We hand the cup and saucer, (or cup and dessert plate) along with a dainty napkin and spoon to the person seated closest to us, while other guests come over to us for their cup. (Of course, fancy paper napkins are acceptable, especially for a large group, but don't you love the feel of linen?) Everyone helps himself to an assortment of tiny sandwiches, dainty muffins or slices of fresh cinnamon toast on pretty little platters. Sweets such as cookies, coffee cakes or brownies, mints or glazed nuts look especially tempting and take up so much less space when they're arranged on two- or three-tiered serving dishes.

A CHIC AND ELEGANT SMALL TEA

Giving a tea party, even a small tea for fifteen or twenty, should be a joyful experience and one should not be trapped in the kitchen refilling the teapot, coffeepot, creamer and replenishing platters! Train your cleaning woman or baby-sitter if necessary, to do these simple chores for you and remind her please to keep an eye on the tea-table during the rush instead of waiting in the kitchen watching the clock! I know it's not easy, but do be firm about this. Or ask a close friend to lend a helping hand during the rush.

When there are more people than the hostess can informally handle herself, it's best to set the tea things on a tray on a large table, such as a dining table from which everyone helps himself to sandwiches and sweets. One or more ladies is given the honor of pouring, never for more than half an hour each, usually fifteen or twenty minutes is enough. With a very large group tea and coffee may be served from both ends of the table to speed the service.

Mrs. Edsel B. Ford overcomes the bane of picked-over platters at her large benefit teas catered at her lakeshore estate in Grosse Pointe, Mich. She uses numerous 10-inch plates which are easy to pass in the crowd, especially with hot tidbits, and are quickly refilled. Worth remembering.

TEA TALK

Whether you serve hot tea or iced tea is up to you, but no tea bags, please! Select a good brand of loose tea flavored perhaps with orange and spice if you like, and brew it properly in a preheated teapot. Then let the conversation flow . . . hot and spicy as the tea!

BREWING A GOOD CUP OF TEA

There are four golden rules tea-lovers from Ceylon to San Francisco agree should be followed.

1. Preheat the teapot with boiling water.

2. For full flavor, bring fresh cold water to a full rolling boil. (Water that has been preheated in a kettle gives tea a flat taste.)

3. Empty hot water from teapot and measure one teaspoon of tea in pot for each cup of hot water.

4. Allow to brew in the pot from three to five minutes before pouring.

Elegant Small Tea

Assorted Mini-sandwiches   Open-faced Sandwiches
Toasted Mushroom Triangles
London Tea Squares   Open Apple Cake
Spiced Tea   Coffee
Mints, Nuts
(Sandwich recipes are together at the end of this chapter)

LONDON TEA SQUARES

If you can manage to do a little quick and easy baking on the morning of your tea, London Tea Squares are as delicate a sweet as you'll find anywhere. The pastry is covered with a thin layer of jam and topped with meringue and sprinkled with nuts. (I wish I could tell you they keep, but they're best eaten within hours!)

    2 cups all-purpose flour
    1/4 teaspoon soda

1 teaspoon vanilla
1/4 cup skimmed milk
1/4 pound butter, room temp.
1/4 cup sugar
3 egg yolks
1 cup of your favorite jam

For meringue

3 egg whites
1/2 cup sugar
1/8 cup of your favorite nuts, chopped.

Preheat oven 350°F. Sift flour (even presifted flour) once in a small bowl and then add soda. Combine vanilla and milk in a cup. In a medium size bowl, cream butter and 1/4 cup sugar. Add egg yolks and beat until light. Add flour alternately with milk and blend thoroughly. Pat dough into a 9 x 13 in. pan to 1/4 in. thickness and spread with jam. Beat egg whites until frothy and add sugar gradually and beat until egg whites come to a point. Spread meringue over jam and sprinkle with chopped nuts. Bake in 350°F oven for 25 minutes. Cool and cut in small 2 in. squares or rectangles. Makes about 25 little pieces.

OPEN APPLE PIE

My all-time favorite tea pastry, because it's so—well, elegantly feminine—so lovely to look at, is a glazed open fresh apple pie. When the apples are arranged as directed in an overlapping circular pattern the pie looks like a golden chrysanthemum. (This too is best served fresh and should not be made the day before.) Serve with forks.

1/4 pound butter, room temp.
1 cup flour
1 package (4 oz.) cream cheese, room temp.
Dash of salt
8 medium apples
2 tablespoons sugar
1/4 teaspoon cinnamon
2 tablespoons lemon juice
1/2 cup apple jelly

This recipe will make two open apple pies in 9 in. layer cake pans. One for your tea and one for the freezer.

1. Cut butter into small pieces. Mix by hand with flour until absorbed. Add cheese and salt and mix by hand until smooth. Put in refrigerator overnight or chill in freezer for 2 hours.

2. Preheat oven to 450°F. Flour board well and roll dough with floured rolling pin until less than 1/4 in. thin.

3. Place dough on bottom of 9 in. layer cake pans or spring form and cut away excess dough from edge. (Do not flour or butter cake pans.) With a fork, puncture holes in dough about 30 times. Take bottom pan (we don't need the rim) and put in oven for 10 minutes.

4. Quarter apples and slice evenly in 1/8 in. wedges. Remove pie pan from oven and place wedges in overlapping circular pattern. Sprinkle with cinnamon and sugar mixed together, add lemon juice and bake for 15 or 20 minutes in 450° oven until apples puff.

5. Cool and glaze by pouring 1/4 cup melted apple jelly over pie. Serve at room temperature. Each pie makes 10 servings.

A BONNIE DEVONSHIRE TEA

"Much may be made of a Scotchman if he be caught young."
Dr. Samuel Johnson

Catching a young fellow today isn't any easier than it was two hundred years ago, especially if he's under twenty-one, for parents who are anxious to give a homecoming party in a state where liquor can't be served to those under that magical age. (New York and Louisiana permit sale of alcoholic beverages to persons over 18 years of age. In Hawaii the age is 20. A few states allow the sale of beer only to those under 21).

Our club, like many private clubs and organizations, wished to entertain for the young college set during vacation, but the entertainment committee's hands were tied with an age group that's too mature for bubble-gum and too young for beer!

We solved this dilemma by sponsoring a Devonshire Tea featuring those heavenly Scottish scones, a kind of super biscuit. Both lads and lassies were invited at 4:30 in the afternoon to the golf club, an ideal masculine setting, for you'll recall that the game of golf originated in Scotland. The Devonshire Tea is the counterpart of our American cocktail party—but no alcohol is served. Oh, 'tis a bonnie affair, ne'ertheless! Instead of the more traditional string orchestra, the committee engaged a talented young folk singer with an electric guitar, and before long the rafters were ringing with song, while some people took "the high road" and others "the low road" and half the group got to Scotland 'afore anyone else!

The committee set up a long buffet table in the center of the room accessible to everyone from all sides, covered with a bright red, green and white plaid cloth. For a centerpiece we used a large copper teakettle filled with flowering thistle (allowing the florist plenty of time to order the flowers). Because tea-table centerpieces should always be high, the arrangement was elevated on a 12-inch base also draped with scotch plaid material and trimmed with branches of scotch pine, the tips lightly sprayed gold. A dozen tall green candles set in teacups trimmed with sprigs of scotch pine circled the centerpiece.

Getting back to the menu, originally scones were served with clotted cream, a specialty of Devonshire County, England, but cream cheese is usually substituted nowadays. Members of the clan split their own scones, first spreading them with soft cream cheese, mixed with a little sour cream if one likes, and strawberry preserves. It's also fun dipping fresh strawberries, with stems attached, in sour cream sweetened with sugar, or in just plain powdered sugar.

Devonshire Tea Menu

Assorted Mini-Sandwiches   Open-faced Sandwiches
Scotch Scones
Scottish Smoked Salmon
on Party Rye
Strawberry, Blackberry, Orange Preserves
Fresh Strawberries
with
Powdered Sugar
Assorted Nuts   Tea   Licorice Mints

Fresh Scottish smoked salmon is flown directly from Scotland via New York to any city in the United States. Epicures (millionaire-type and generous!) can order 6 lbs (serves about 100) for $55. The fish goes a long way and should be sliced almost flat and as paper-thin as possible and eaten at room temperature. (See Sources of Supply)

However, if you live near the Great Lakes, new plantings of co-ho salmon are now revolutionizing the commercial fishing industry. Co-ho salmon sells in this area around $1 a lb. and smoked co-ho is marvelous. Do watch for it at your local market soon.

Or you may substitute lox from your delicatessen store, or prepare a dandy spread from canned salmon.

Invitation for a Devonshire Tea:

Lads and Lassies—
> *Let's go to a Devonshire Tea*
> *(Don't be a fool, Mac, it's free!)*
> *There'll be music on bones*
> *With lots of hot hot scones*
> *4:30 is the time for our spree.*

SCOTCH SCONES

Scotch scones are served hot like biscuits and there are some ready-mixes on the market, but in case you'd like to make your own here's a tasty recipe. (We love them with Chicken Fricassée or turkey salad too!)

    2 cups all-purpose flour
    4 teaspoons baking powder
    2 teaspoons sugar
    1/2 teaspoon salt
    4 tablespoons butter
    2 eggs
    1/3 cup cream
    Sugar-cinnamon mixture: 1/4 teaspoon cinnamon and
        2 tablespoons sugar

Preheat oven to 400°F. Mix and sift flour, baking powder, sugar, salt in large bowl. Cut in butter and mix to consistency of coarse cornmeal. Add well beaten eggs and cream. Turn on lightly floured board, pat and roll to 1/2 in. thickness and cut into diamonds about 2 inches wide or into small triangles. Brush with a little egg white and sprinkle with sugar-cinnamon mixture and place on floured baking sheet. Bake for 15 minutes. Makes 12 scones.

Addenda: One may expand the Scotch menu by including additional native items such as trout and herring along with superb Angus or Aberdeen beef, venison and grouse.

EASTER SUNDAY TEA FOR CHILDREN
AND GROWN-UPS

One lovely year our anniversary fell on Easter Sunday, so my husband and I decided to invite some close relatives and friends with their children to an Easter Sunday tea party.

At about three-thirty, five or six families arrived on a cool but sunny day, and to everyone's surprise and delight there was a real-live welcoming rabbit in our living room! (He was quite safe in a sturdy playpen covered with chicken wire.) The gimmick for this afternoon's entertainment was to have each child draw an egg from a nest of hardcooked colored Easter eggs, on which we'd inscribed every child's name—twelve children, twelve eggs, twelve names. The child who drew his own name first would win the rabbit as his very own to keep, and we didn't need much else in the way of entertainment. Every child present hoped he'd be the lucky one to take the live bunny home, and every parent present hoped somebody else's child would be the "lucky" one!

In the family room we set up two large bridge tables with portable round tops for six children each, and we covered the tables with brightly flowered print cloths. In the center of the table we filled a basket with small favors from the dime store, and tied animal shaped balloons filled with helium to the handles. We gave each child a small tray, cafeteria style, on which he could put his mug of hot chocolate, sandwiches, cookies and cake.

Grown-ups served themselves from a buffet spread on the dining room table, which was covered with a matching flowered print and in the center stood a spring arrangement of hyacinth in a pastel wicker basket. But before the grand drawing, we fortified the adults with a welcome cup of hot tea spiked with a spoonful of flaming orange curaçao.

Easter Sunday Tea Menu

Watercress Sandwich   Cucumber Sandwich
Pimento Cheese Carrots on Crackers
Peanut-Butter and Jelly Sandwich
Minced Chicken Sandwich
Petit Pecan Rolls
Fudge Cake
Snow Balls or Lamb Cake from cake mold
Easter Egg Candies
Orange Curaçao Tea
Hot Chocolate with Marshmallow Topping

FUDGE CAKE

This treasured family recipe from my friend Vi Ranger, is quick, easy and very rich, just the kind most children as well as grown-ups adore.

1 cup butter, room temp.
2 cups sugar
4 whole eggs beaten together
1 cup cake flour
1 cup walnuts, chopped fine
1 teaspoon vanilla

Icing

1 tablespoon butter, melted
3 tablespoon cocoa
2 cups powdered sugar
1 teaspoon vanilla
1/4 cup hot water

1. Preheat oven to 400°F. In a large mixing bowl mix butter with sugar until fluffy. Add well beaten eggs alternating with flour. Add walnuts and vanilla.

2. Bake cake in shallow pan, 8 x 12 inches, for 20 to 25 minutes. Get icing ready while cake is baking and spread over cake the minute you take the cake from the oven. If icing is too stiff, just add a little more hot water. Makes 24 small pieces.

PECAN ROLLS OR SCHNECKEN

Individual pecan rolls or schnecken are made with yeast. If you've never tried baking with yeast this rich dough is well worth the initial effort. You can make them any size you like from 1 1/2 in. to 3 in. round depending on the size muffin tin you use. They're best served warm and freeze beautifully. They can be prepared in two steps on successive days or all in one day if you start early in the morning.

Pecan rolls are good for breakfast, lunch, tea, or served with coffee as dessert after a cocktail supper. (The dough can be used for rolls, stollen or fruit ring.)

Dough

    2 packages yeast
    1 cup warm milk
    1 cup butter
    2 eggs
    4 tablespoon sugar
    1 teaspoon salt
    4 cups all-purpose flour (no sifting necessary)

Soak yeast in half a cup of warm milk for 15 minutes. Melt the butter in rest of the milk. Beat eggs with sugar, salt, and combine with yeast mixture. Add four cups unsifted flour, beat well. Cover dough with a clean dish cloth and let rise in a warm place for 5 to 6 hours. You may put the dough in the refrigerator overnight covered, but if you do be sure to let the dough and bowl reach room temperature and allow to rise again when you take it out of the refrigerator the next day.

Filling

    1 cup melted butter
    1 cup sugar mixed with 1 tablespoon cinnamon
    1 or 1 1/2 cups raisins
    1 1/4 cups chopped pecans
    2 cups of pecan halves

Take 1/3 of the dough and roll on a floured board with a floured rolling pin to 1/4 thickness. Brush with melted butter, sprinkle with sugar, cinnamon, chopped pecans and raisins. Roll the dough over once and brush with melted butter. Repeat until you have a nice long roll like a jelly roll. With a sharp knife cut into one-inch pieces.

Syrup

    1/4 pound butter
    1 cup dark brown sugar
    2 tablespoons water
Melt butter, add sugar and water and cook until thick.

Assembly

Preheat oven to 350°F. Brush muffin pan with melted butter, fill each container with about 1 tablespoon syrup, and 2 or 3 pecans. Place rolls on top, brush with melted butter, and let rise for about half an hour or until puffy. Repeat until all dough is used. Bake in 350° oven for twenty minutes or until brown. Invert pan, remove Pecan Rolls and cool on rack, serve caramel side up. Best eaten warm. Makes 2 dozen.

FLAMING ORANGE CURACAO TEA

Use a black tea and it's best if tea is not too strong. Pour Curaçao into a teaspoon and hold over tea to warm for about a minute. Then light and gently lower spoon into tea and stir.

SNOW BALLS

Follow directions on package of 1 package white cake mix. For three dozen snowballs cut entire cake into 1 1/2 inch squares. (For one dozen snowballs use only 1/3 of cake). Each square after it's covered with icing and shredded coconut makes a 3 in. snowball.

Icing for 1 Dozen Snowballs

    2 cups sugar
    2/3 cup water
    2 tablespoon light corn syrup
    2 egg whites
    1/8 teaspoon salt
    1 1/2 teaspoons vanilla

Cook sugar, water and corn syrup over low heat until sugar is dissolved. Boil without stirring to 238° or until icing forms a soft ball when dropped into a small bowl of cold water. When sugar syrup is almost ready, beat egg whites with salt until stiff but not dry. Pour hot syrup over egg whites in a fine stream, beating constantly. Add vanilla and continue beating until frosting is of spreading consistency.

Coconut

For 1 dozen snowballs use 4 cans 3 1/2 oz. of shredded or flaked coconut or 1 fresh coconut (2 lbs. yields 14 oz. shredded coconut). Using canned coconut flakes is a convenience but grinding a fresh coconut tastes better and is infinitely cheaper.

To break open fresh coconut see Chapter VI.

Grate by hand and spread in a shallow pan.

Assembling Snowballs

Drop individual squares one at a time into icing, coating cake on all sides. With a large spoon, scoop out iced cake and roll lightly in coconut flakes. With your hands pat additional coconut and form into a perfect snowball. Makes 1 dozen snowballs.

VIENNESE STRUDEL TEA

Sometimes a tea becomes memorable simply from hearing about it—this is the case with a Strudel Tea a friend of mine gave in behalf of one of her favorite charities. Nothing else was served but an assortment of Viennese Strudel; apple, apricot, cherry, plum all garnished with generous dabs of real whipped cream.

They tell me there were merry violins playing those marvelous Strauss waltzes among potted palms (rented, of course.) Guests sat at those dear little café tables and chairs (also rented) lost in a world of lace handkerchiefs, duels of honor and romance.

Strudels can be bought ready-made at some bakeries or frozen at your super market. In our house it's more fun to tease mother into making one. For an extra large strudel she always clears the dining room table, covers it with a fresh white table cloth and rolls the dough as far as possible. Now begins the delicate pulling of the dough with light fingertips until it is almost transparently thin right up to the very edge. Please don't panic if a few holes appear because the dough is all rolled together with apples, nuts and raisins anyway into a long loaf.

MOTHER'S VIENNESE APFEL STRUDEL

Dough

2 cups flour
2 eggs
1/2 teaspoon salt
2 tablespoons cold water
1/4 cup Crisco (or olive oil)
1/4 cup lukewarm water

Filling

5 lbs. apples
1 cup chopped walnuts
1 cup white raisins
1/2 cup sugar
2 teaspoons cinnamon
1/4 pound butter, melted
1/4 cup powdered sugar

1. Sift flour into a medium-size bowl and make a well in center. In a separate bowl, stir 2 eggs mixed with salt water and melted Crisco. Add to flour and keep stirring until smooth. Remove from bowl and knead dough into a ball. Bounce dough on table several times until there are no more air bubbles. Form into ball and place on a floured plate. Pat lukewarm water on top of dough so the top does not dry. Cover with bowl and let stand for 1/2 hour or more.

2. Slice apples into thin wedges. Chop nuts, medium fine, add raisins, sugar, and cinnamon and combine with apples in a separate bowl.

3. Spread a tablecloth over large kitchen or dinette table. Sprinkle with flour and roll the dough with a floured rolling pin until very thin. Dust hands with flour, then start pulling dough by sliding hands under dough and lifting from center. With fingertips very gently tease and stretch dough until paper thin all the way to the edges. With a scissor cut away thick edge that may be left.

4. Preheat oven to 350°F. Brush melted butter over dough; sprinkle half the apple mixture all over dough. Lift tablecloth at

one end and flip strudel allowing air bubbles to form in roll. Keep adding apple mixture until it is all used.

5. Place strudel which now looks like a large loaf in a well-'buttered shallow pan about 11" x 16" or on a large well-buttered cookie sheet in a 350° oven for 1 hour or until gold. When strudel has cooled, sprinkle lightly with powdered sugar and serve at room temperature. Makes 8 to 10 servings.

CHAMPAGNE TEA

Staging a tea in honor of a debutante or to announce an engagement or to honor a bride is about as nice an assignment as one can dream of anytime.

Let's think pink because most young ladies prefer pink above any other color. Let's think music because most girls love to be serenaded. Let's think ruffles and velvet bows and flowers, because most girls love doo-dads. Let's think champagne because this is a once-in-a-lifetime affair! Let's think about reading tea leaves because most girls love to dream of the future! Pink, music, ruffles, bows, velvet, flowers, champagne, gypsy fortune tellers—mix them all together and you have a gala champagne tea that will be remembered a lifetime.

The prime focus of this party is a lavishly decorated table about 8 feet long or a large round table is pretty too, covered first with a pink petticoat and then a cloth of nylon net. With a rectangular table it's fun to gather the net in each corner into a pouf by pinning it with a straight florist's pin. The pouf is bound with dark green or blue velvet ribbon tied in a lush bow with long streamers. In addition the net can be trimmed with artificial small cloth flowers that are either lightly pinned or stitched to the net. (See Chapter VIII for more table decorating ideas).

When the challenge of giving a bridal tea was put to me, the image of rococo cherubs and pink roses and dreamy maidens languishing under a tree came to mind. (Luckily my mother-in-law let me borrow her Dresden ornament for this special occasion.) Two tall epergnes filled with baby pink roses and Bristol fairy flowers—similar to baby's breath—flanked the centerpiece.

While party shopping for paper napkins in a gift shop, I found a hanging scroll designed for guest signatures, and the bride thought it was a lovely sentimental souvenir of the day. (It's simple to make a scroll by using two strips of wooden dowels 15" each obtainable at any hardware store. Glue a roll of heavy shelf paper, as long or as short as one wants, around the dowel at each end. Re-enforce the edge of the shelf paper with mastic tape to prevent tearing. To hang scroll, add a braid or silk ribbon attached to the back of the dowel with two screw eyes. If one is artistically inclined, the scroll could be further decorated with ink sketches or decals. Start the ball rolling by signing your name first.)

To honor the bride, I ordered flowered party mints with the young couple's name from my favorite candy store.

Champagne Tea

Hot Mushroom Triangles   Hot Cheese Rolls
Hot Lobster Canapès
Merry-go-round Sandwich   Stuffed Cherry tomatoes
Open-faced Sandwiches: Cold Turkey, Ham, Tongue
Silver Champagne Punch (see Chapter III)
Petit Fours   Cream Puffs
Crispy Lace Cookies
Tea   Coffee
Flower Mints

CRISPY LACE COOKIES

What could be more suitable for a Champagne tea than crisp lace cookies so delicate one can peek through them? They can be made days ahead and keep very well. Lace cookies may be served flat or shaped into cones while still warm. Men adore them too!

2/3 cup packaged almonds
1/4 pound butter
Dash of salt
1/2 cup sugar
1 tablespoon all-purpose flour
2 tablespoons milk

1. Preheat oven to 350°F. Grind almonds medium fine.
2. Melt butter in medium size skillet. Add salt, sugar, flour and stir over flame with wooden spoon until sugar melts. Add milk and almonds, continue to blend until mixture is thick and no longer runny.
3. Use rubber spatula and drop 1 teaspoon dough on buttered and floured cookie sheet 3 in. apart as cookies spread out flat. (Remove skillet from stove and cover. It's best to use 2 cookie sheets, medium size, and make cookies quickly as the dough has a tendency to dry out.) Re-flour and butter cookie sheet each time.
4. Bake in oven for about 10 minutes and remove from oven; let cool for 2 minutes before removing from cookie sheet with spatula. Place cookies on cooling rack and they will become nice and crisp. Or they can be shaped into cones while still warm.

ASSORTED MINI-SANDWICHES

There are a few simple rules to follow in making not only attractive but tasty fresh mini-sandwiches.
1. If you avoid combining all cream cheese recipes with bread your battle's already won. In my opinion, cream cheese on soft white or whole wheat bread is about as tasty as Elmer's glue! Tinting the cheese pink or green and mixing it with chopped olives or nuts doesn't help the texture either. (Cream cheese is good only as a spread on crisp crackers, chips, brown bread or biscuits.)

2. Use thinly sliced white, whole wheat and rye bread. Spread bread lightly with softened butter to prevent the filling from soaking into bread.

3. Use an "assembly line" technique with plenty of counter top space for cutting and spreading sandwiches.

4. Certain types of sandwiches can be prepared in advance and frozen, but fillings containing hard-cooked egg whites, raw vegetables and mayonnaise *do not* freeze successfully.

5: Use a sharp knife for trimming edges and cutting bread or it will tear.

6. One cup of filling will spread about 5 dozen mini-sandwiches.

7. To estimate the number of sandwiches and other tidbits for teas or receptions, it's a safe rule to provide five pieces for each guest, regardless of the number of varieties served. (For cocktails allow a minimum of seven pieces because drinking promotes appetite for hors d'oeuvres.)

If three cups of filling make 15 dozen mini-sandwiches allow about 3 hours to make 180 sandwiches from scratch. Of course the job goes faster with someone to work along with you and keep you company. Making sandwiches can be broken down into stages.

The day before: Make the fillings. Spread the ribbon sandwiches and wrap whole after cutting. They will stay fresh and moist in Saran wrap.

The day of the party. Open-faced sandwiches are best made fresh in the morning on the day of the party. Put them on a serving tray or platter and cover with a damp-dry towel and then cover with Saran wrap.

SANDWICH SPREADS

The following three basic sandwich spreads taste delicious separately or blend well together between alternate layers of white, whole wheat and rye bread; 1) yellow cheese 2) Braunschweiger liver sausage and 3) chopped egg mixture.

There's an infinite variety of sandwiches to be had when combining three kinds of spread with three types of bread and cutting the bread into various shapes (circles, squares, triangles) plus making open-faced sandwiches that in turn can be cut with a variety of cookie cutters into heart shapes, tree shapes, spades, clubs or diamonds and finally decorated with a sliver of olive, a strip of pimento or a sprig of parsley.

Two layer sandwiches can be cut either crisscross into small squares and triangles while three layer or ribbon sandwiches are made by alternating rye, liver-sausage spread, whole wheat, chopped egg spread, white bread, cheese spread and rye or in any combination one would wish. With a very sharp knife, trim the edges of the sandwich then cut the bread in four parallel strips.

Yellow Cheese Mixture

    1/2 pound medium sharp store cheese
    3 strips red pimento for color
    1/4 cup mayonnaise
    1 teaspoon minced onion

With a hand food chopper cut cheese and mix with pimento, mayonnaise, and onion until smooth; makes 1 1/2 cups.

Braunschweiger Liver-sausage Mixture

> 1 package 8 oz. Braunschweiger liver sausage
> 1/4 cup mayonnaise
> 1/4 cup sweet pickle relish

With a hand food chopper cut liver-sausage and add mayonnaise and pickle relish and mix until smooth. Makes 1 1/2 cups.

Chopped Egg Mixture

> 3 hard-boiled eggs
> 1/4 cup mayonnaise
> 1 teaspoon dried parsley flakes
> 1 tablespoon finely chopped fresh onion, (less if you don't care for onion flavor)
> 2 tablespoon chopped celery, very fine
> salt and pepper to taste

With hand food chopper, chop eggs. Add mayonnaise, parsley, onion, celery, salt and pepper and mix until smooth. Makes 2 cups.

PIMENTO CHEESE CARROTS

> 1 jar (5 oz.) Pimento cheese spread
> 1 package 4 oz. grated Cheddar cheese
> White oval cracker

Mix cheddar with pimento. Make carrots using 1 teaspoon of mix to each carrot and roll into shape. Garnish top with sprig of parsley and place one tiny carrot on a oval, white cracker. Makes 50 carrots.

WATERCRESS SANDWICH

> 1/3 cup finely chopped watercress

2 tablespoons mayonnaise
Dash of salt, pepper and paprika
whole watercress for garnishing

Mix watercress and mayonnaise into a paste.

Cut fresh bread into very thin slices and remove crust. Spread with watercress paste and roll. Optional: insert sprig of fresh watercress at one end before rolling for garnish.

Makes 2 dozen mini-sandwiches.

MINCED CHICKEN SANDWICH

Let's not disguise that solid, good chicken flavor with any sharp mayonnaise, celery or spices. For all we know, we could be eating tuna fish most of the time and never taste the difference. Much better to hear people saw, "Mmmmm, that tastes like chicken."

(See recipe for cooking chicken or turkey in Chapter II.)

1 cup shredded white meat of chicken or turkey. Add just enough prepared whipped topping to bind chicken into a paste. Spread between white bread and cut in squares. (Low in calories, too!) Makes 5 dozen mini-sandwiches.

TOASTED MUSHROOM SANDWICHES

1 cup chopped mushrooms
1 tablespoon butter
1/4 teaspoon salt
3/4 cup condensed cream of mushroom soup (not
    diluted)
Dash of nutmeg

Sauté chopped mushrooms in a small skillet with butter until golden. Add salt. Remove from skillet and mix with soup and nutmeg. Preheat oven to 475°F. Spread on very thin slices of white bread (trimmed) and toast in oven for about 5 minutes or until brown. Cut crisscross into four squares or triangles. Makes 40 sandwiches.

HOT TOASTED CHEESE ROLLS

Make the filling the day before the sandwiches are to be served. Chill overnight.

1 tablespoon flour
1/4 teaspoon Worcestershire sauce
1/4 teaspoon mustard
1/2 teaspoon salt
Dash of red pepper
1 cup milk
1 cup grated sharp American cheese
4 egg yolks, beaten
Dash of Tabasco sauce

Combine flour and seasonings except Tabasco. Add milk slowly to make a smooth paste and cook in double boiler until thickened. Add cheese and stir until melted and sauce is smooth. Beat yolks, add Tabasco and pour part of the hot mixture into beaten egg yolk then return egg mixture to double boiler. Cook for a minute longer and remove from heat. Chill overnight. On the day of the party warm cheese to room temperature for easy spreading on thin slices of fresh bread with crust removed. Roll cheese and bread and toast under broiler for a few minutes or until cheese melts and toast turns gold. Serve hot by passing on platters covered with paper lace doilies. Makes 4 dozen rolls.

CUCUMBER SANDWICH

2 medium size cucumbers
2 teaspoons salt
Bottled mayonnaise with horseradish or 1 tablespoon
    horseradish mixed into 1 cup mayonnaise

Pare and slice cucumber very fine. Taste raw cucumber to see if it's bitter. Once in awhile one does get a bitter cucumber and it's best to buy an extra one just in case this should happen . Sprinkle with 2 teaspoons salt and let stand for several hours in refrigerator. Drain water. Use very, very thin white bread, or cut regular slice in half horizontally. Spread with thin layer of horseradish-mayonnaise and cucumbers. Cover with bread and gently press together. Trim edge of bread and cut in half. Keep cool until serving. Makes 40 sandwiches.

MERRY-GO-ROUND PIE

The Merry-go-round sandwich truly appeals to the eye as well as the palate. It can be served at receptions and cocktail parties as well as teas. All ingredients are prepared ahead of time, leaving just the assembling for the last hour. A genuine work of art—an assemblage!

For this you need a round 9″ uncut rye bread which you can order from the baker or find at your supermarket. Coax him to slice it for you through the very center, horizontally, in several slices. (If you have a chef's knife at home, you can manage it yourself)

For two Merry-Go-Round sandwiches (cut into 12 pie-shaped slices each) you need:

    4 hard-cooked eggs
    3 tablespoons mayonnaise
    1/2 teaspoon salt
    1/4 teaspoon dry mustard
    1/8 tablespoon cayenne pepper
    2 tablespoons sour cream
    10 chopped black pitted olives
    2 cans boned sardines
    1 lemon
    1/8 pound butter
    1 four-ounce jar red caviar

Prepare hard-cooked eggs. Mash yolks and mix with mayonnaise seasoned with salt, mustard and cayenne pepper. Chop 2 of the egg whites and mix with sour cream, separately. Chop black olives, medium fine, separately. Mince sardines with juice of 1/2 lemon, separately.

Remove crust from sliced bread and spread with softened butter. Spread black olives in a dollar-size circle in center of bread. (Optional. You may substitute black caviar for olives) Carefully spread egg yolk mixture in a ring around olives with a knife. Spread red caviar around yellow egg yolk mixture evenly. (Optional. You may substitute devilled ham for red caviar) Spread chopped egg whites around red caviar. Spread minced, boned sardines flavored with lemon juice around red caviar. Garnish platter with sprigs of parsley.

Place whole slice of round rye on platter and cut into 12 pie-shaped pieces with a very sharp knife, leaving the effect of the disk as a whole, decorated with rings of variegated colored spreads.

HOT LOBSTER CANAPE

    1 can (7 1/2 oz.) lobster
    1/4 cup sherry wine
    1/4 cup grated Parmesan cheese
    1/3 cup buttered crumbs
    Paprika

Shred lobster meat, add sherry and cheese. Spread on small rounds of bread in mound. Sprinkle with buttered crumbs and brown lightly in broiler for a few minutes. Sprinkle lightly with paprika. Makes 4 dozen canapés.

STUFFED CHERRY TOMATOES

Slit 1/3 down each cherry tomato and let a little juice flow. Then fill slit with your favorite dip of cottage cheese, cream cheese, pimento, etc. For cocktails use the saltier dips such as anchovy paste and cream cheese, etc. Stuffed cherry tomatoes are tasty and very decorative used as a garnish on platters, too, along with big bunches of parsley.

ICED ORANGE TEA

Any hot summer day, after a fast game of tennis, people like to drop by our house for a refreshing glass of iced tea while we re-hash the trials and triumphs of the morning's sets of mixed doubles.

Our iced-orange-tea recipe, garnished with a sprig of fresh mint from the garden, is also refreshing used as a summer punch with paper-thin sliced lemons and oranges floating on top, garnished with cloves and a sliver of maraschino cherry. The punch is ladled over ice in a glass. For an added kick, reduce amount of orange juice to half and add 1 cup of Triple-Sec Liqueur.

    2 quarts water
    1/2 cup Orange Pekoe and Pekoe Tea
    1/2 cup frozen orange juice concentrate
    2 cups water
    1/2 cup lemon juice
    Garnishes

Bring fresh water to a rolling boil. Add tea and let brew for 5 minutes. Pour tea through a strainer into 3 quart pitcher. (Place a long handled metal spoon in pitcher if it is glass to prevent cracking)

Combine frozen orange juice concentrate with 2 cups water. Add orange juice and lemon juice to tea.

Serve in 8 oz. glasses half filled with ice and garnish with slices of lemon and orange, clove, mint or maraschino cherries. Let guests sweeten with sugar to taste. Makes 16 glasses.

Presentation is a punch's prerequisite! A hot punch served in a brightly gleaming silver bowl or a chilled punch served in a sparkling crystal bowl with a long-handled ladle presented on a round table with matching punch glasses has the sort of eye-appeal that's bound to draw an enthusiastic crowd. (Oh, deliver us from those insipid colored liquids served in paper cups!)

One can even dazzle guests by making a punch bowl from a huge block of ice which weighs anywhere from 25, 50, 100 up to 300 lbs. If ice has been stored at zero degrees, let it stand at room temperature about 20 minutes before you start shaping the bowl. Start hole in top center of block by chipping lightly with a chisel. Be gentle because ice is brittle and has a tendency to split if pounded too hard. Then place a round metal bowl, about 3-quart capacity or more, in the small hole and keep bowl filled with very hot water until the depression is the desired size. When serving, set ice on a tray or shallow pan to hold the small amount of water which melts from the block of ice, or siphon excess water through a hose into a pail hidden under the table. Mask pan with leaves and flowers.

A friend of mine volunteered to serve cocktails at home to a large group of 250 out-of-town delegates before an annual dinner meeting. To help break the ice, literally and figuratively speaking, she served the ever popular martini in a punch bowl! In the center of the bowl she put a large block of ice with a small depression on top for olives and for an added touch of color she surrounded the olives with a wreath of bright flowers. Truly a conversation piece! (Martini recipe in Chapter IV.)

PARTY PUNCH

> 2 cups boiling water
> 4 tablespoons tea leaves (black)
> 3 large lemons
> 2 cups sugar
> 4 cups cold water
> 1 teaspoon vanilla extract
> 1 teaspoon almond extract
> 2 bottles (each 28 oz.) ginger ale
> 1 can pineapple tidbits (frozen)

Pour 2 cups of boiling water over tea leaves; cover and steep for 10 minutes. Wash lemons, extract juice; add sugar, water and lemon rinds and heat, stirring until sugar is dissolved. Strain tea through sieve and add. When mixture is cool, stir in vanilla

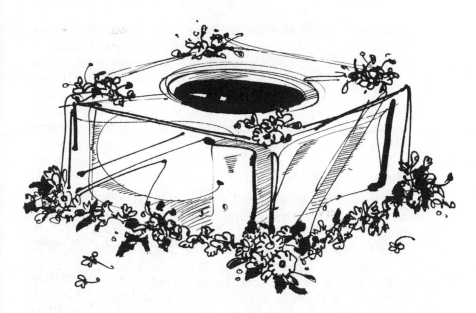

and almond extract. Chill until serving time. Pour into punch bowl and add ginger ale. Float tidbits (frozen in can and removed as cylinder) in punch. Makes 30 cups. (By permission of Hawaiian Visitors Bureau)

FRESH PEACH PUNCH

For a summer wedding—

    3 pounds ripe peaches, sliced
    1/4 cup sugar
    1/4 cup brandy
    1 fifth red wine (chilled)
    1 fifth white wine (chilled)
    1 bottle domestic champagne (chilled)

Add sugar and brandy to peaches and let stand 3 to 4 hours. Place in crystal punch bowl and pour over the red wine and white wine. Keep cold. Add block of ice and just before serving add champagne. Makes 24 servings.

SILVER CHAMPAGNE PUNCH

      3 magnums of domestic champagne
      (a magnum is 2 quarts)
      1 quart Courvoisier
      Several dashes of bitters

Pour over molded ice ring and serve in silver punch bowl. Makes 50 servings, 3 ounces each.

ICED COFFEE

Whenever my husband and I go on a motor trip and we stop off at a roadside restaurant for refreshment during the summer, he always asks the waitress for a glass of iced coffee and she almost always says, "We don't serve that here" to which my husband gently replies, "Very well, just bring me a cup of hot coffee and a glass with ice." This she is both willing and relieved to do and he proceeds to pour the hot coffee into a glass of ice. adding cream and sugar. Iced coffee!

With all the coffee drinking that's done in this country it's hard to understand why it's taken so long for iced coffee to become popular when it's so good! Iced coffee is just as easy to serve to a large group as hot coffee. It's best to make it extra strong, then let it cool before pouring so the ice in the glass doesn't melt too quickly. Sugar and cream or saccharin is up to the individual.

COFFEE KAHLUA

This Mexican coffee variation appeals to many. Just add 1 jigger of Kahlua (a delicious coffee liqueur) to each glass of iced coffee, then top with a dab of whipped cream.

Stop by for a Drink!

Count Metterlink, of the blue-bird-of-happiness fame, was ninety years of age when he was invited to attend a New York cocktail party where he commented, "It is better to be ninety years young than to be forty years old!"

THE COCKTAIL PARTY RITUAL:

A cocktail party can be as intimate as a throbbing violin or as noisy as a brass band. Is can be as impromptu as "Drop over for a drink" or as formal as an engraved invitation. It can include no more than a handful or a house full! The cocktail party at its best is as American as iced coffee, as tempting as a hot dog and as noisy as a ball game. You can be bored one minute and deeply engrossed the next. You can be too hot or cold, drink too much, eat too little and go home too late. But the cocktail party ritual is as habit-forming as reading the Sunday paper, and though you may not care for today's headlines, you can't ignore them any more than you can ignore the next warm invitation for a small libation.

R.S.P.V.'s:

No matter whether you give a cocktail party for fun, or to raise funds, there are two points worth remembering when writing invitations that generally don't apply at other times. First, set the exact hour the party is expected to begin and end. This is a welcome bit of information every guest wants to know (and should abide by). For example; from 5:00 to 7:00, or 5:30 to 7:30, or 6:00 to 8:00, or 5:00 to 9:00 if you like! There are times you might not care if your friends want to stay and s-t-a-y, drinking their dinner, but then again don't feel it's necessary to urge people to stay just to be polite. When they say, "Well, we've got to be running along"—let them run!

The second point involves a recent trend for written invitations and that is simply writing R.S.V.P. above the words "Regrets Only", or the tongue-in-cheek R.S.S.V.N.P.V. (*Répondez seulement si vous ne pouves pas venir!*) Or putting it positively, some hostesses prefer the phrase, "Acceptances Only". Either way, this grass-roots movement has not been officially acknowledged in etiquette books, but there's a good chance it may catch hold, simply because it cuts down on the deluge of phone calls which follows the mailing of a large batch of invitations. It's unfortunate that only a minority ever troubles itself to send written notes of acceptance or regrets, so perhaps we should be open to change whether we like it or not. Manners, like language, undergo constant adjustment, bending with the stress and strain of our times. "It's me" is considered quite acceptable by the majority of linguists today because the grammatically proper "it is I" sounds artificial to our ears. But getting back to invitations, there is another alternative and that is simply eliminating the request for R.S.V.P.'s entirely (which one can do for an Open House) but—that does leave one hanging, doesn't it?

OPEN-HOUSE COCKTAIL PARTY:

Our last cocktail party for over a hundred was the easiest, most successful and therefore my favorite! The date—a Saturday in January, the time 5:00 to 9:00, the occasion—to celebrate our newly remodeled kitchen.

In the past, we've always been cramped for space, but now we decided to feature our remodeled pride and joy by turning our square kitchen into a bar. For once, there's ample counter space for making drinks, for ice, liquor, mixes, glasses, etc.! Running water is always handy and used glasses are quickly whisked out of sight and deposited in the dishwasher.

Fortunately we'd selected kitchen carpeting which cuts down on the noise, and our new cove lighting under the hanging cabinets makes glasses sparkle. Our oven fans conveniently draw out cigarette smoke and a braided string of red onions hanging from our beamed ceiling adds a nice touch of color. We were surprised and delighted to discover that our functional, attractive, spacious kitchen now serves a dual purpose. (Architects, please note!)

A successful party has to breathe, to flow, and the vitality of a party, like physical well-being, often depends on good circulation. Guests like to move about freely, to wander over to the bar for more ice, or to stop by the hors d'oeuvres table for a snack, or to pause in front of a cozy fire; people don't like being trapped in corners for the entire evening. Avoid bottlenecks throughout the house such as setting up a portable bar in the hallway—this space is better reserved solely for arriving and departing guests.

We've learned from experience when entertaining a large group it's best to eliminate dainty chairs and tippy tables, and since we don't have a magnificent view through our windows at night, we always draw the draperies, giving our living room an intimate, congenial atmosphere. We build a crackling fire in the living-room fireplace where changing groups sit comfortably with plenty of ash trays scattered about on numerous occasional tables.

In the dining area, the hors d'oeuvre table is moved against the wall to give us additional room. On this occasion we used an arrangement of colorful fruit; pineapple, avocados, apples, grapes, limes and pomegranates sliced in half. We added a group of assorted candles of various colors and sizes at one end of the table —big fat ones and short chunky ones.

When planning the menu for a cocktail party, it's simplest to divide foods into four basic groups: 1) cheese, 2) seafood, 3) meat, 4) vegetables. These in turn are divided into two sub-groups—hot and cold. This done, we're off to a good running start! The paradox in planning, however, is; the more variety—the fancier, but sometimes the fancier the food—the less variety! For instance, one could offer nothing but the finest selection of imported cheeses from France, Holland, Denmark, Norway, Italy, etc., which could be served whole, sliced, cubed, or creamed with an assortment of rye bread and crackers. Or nothing but fresh seafood—oysters and caviar!

Our Open-House menu was chosen carefully, because we didn't want to mess up the kitchen by cooking or broiling on the day of the party, nor did I wish to be on my feet all day, so everything was prepared the day before, leaving the kitchen (and me) bright and sparkling.

Open-House Menu
Liederkranz Ring Mold
Hot Cheese Cookies   Imported Swiss Cheese
Smoked Virginia Ham
Marinade Cubed Beef Over Hibachi
Liver Pate   Michigan Smoked Fish
Assorted Crackers   Party Rye
Fresh Pineapple Chunks on toothpicks
Dipped in Powdered Sugar
Mocha Coffee

PEANUTS—POP-CORN AND PRETZELS:

Why oh why do some hostesses delay serving as much as a pretzel during the early cocktail hour until *all* the guests have arrived? This could mean a pretty long wait until the last straggler has made his appearance so why penalize the punctual guest this way? At least set a bowl of nuts, potato chips, or fritos for those who've perhaps made the supreme effort to be on time in spite of a flooded basement or a long distance telephone call or a missing puppy!

Liederkranz Ring Mold

    5 packages (four-ounce each) Liederkranz cheese
    1 cup domestic dry white wine
    1 1/4 pounds sweet butter, softened
    1/3 cup brandy

Put cheese in a bowl and pour wine over to cover, and soak overnight. In the morning, drain cheese, add sweet butter and mash well together. When well blended, add 1/3 cup brandy, mix and put in mold and chill in refrigerator. To remove from ring mold before serving, place platter over ring mold and turn upside down. (If necessary, place hot wet towels on ring mold and shake platter and ring mold gently, until Liederkranz cheese falls free.) Serves 20.

Hot Cheese Cookies

These are made like ice-box cookies. Cheese cookies can be made ahead and freeze very well. They're just as good when reheated and may be served warm or cold. We like to keep them warm on an electric hot tray, but they're gobbled up so quickly, it's not easy!

    1 cup grated sharp American cheese
    1 cup grated medium sharp American cheese
    1 cup flour
    1/2 cup butter, softened
    1/4 teaspoon cayenne pepper

1. Grate cheese, medium fine, on sheet of wax paper. Put cheese in large mixing bowl and add flour, butter, and cayenne pepper. Mix well together by hand and divide into 2 balls.

2. Put each ball on a separate sheet of wax paper and fold paper over dough. Using the wax paper, form into 2 rolls, each 1 1/2 inch in diameter. (The wax paper keeps the dough from sticking to your hands.) Place rolled dough with wax paper overnight in refrigerator. (For quickie results, put in freezer for 2 hours instead.)

3. Preheat oven to 400°F. and remove dough when hard from refrigerator. Peel off wax paper and slice in 1/4-inch thickness. Lightly grease cookie sheet (the first time only) and place

cookies 1/2-inch apart on cookie sheet. Bake for 12 minutes, or until cookies are pale gold. Repeat until all cookies are done. Yield 8 dozen.

SMOKED VIRGINIA HAM

Three hundred years ago, aristocratic European families were captivated by the rich, succulent, sweet nutlike flavor of Virginia hams, and our guests are just as captivated today. It takes almost a year to smoke and age this meat to perfection, but the wait is well worth the result.

For a large cocktail party, I usually order one smoked ham (See Sources of Supply). This is delivered by mail, fully cooked, ready to serve hot or cold (We prefer it cold). A 10- or 15-lb. ham, sliced paper thin and served with party rye, will go a long way at your next party.

FUN WITH FIRE

To serve food piping hot at a cocktail party, or brunch or buffet supper, one needs an accessory or two, such as a chafing dish, a fondue set, a hibachi charcoal burner, or an electric gadget. One couldn't possibly own, let alone store, all the different items available on today's market. We must decide which is the handiest accessory for us and then become proficient in our own delightful specialty. A friend of mine uses a portable electric roaster for making miniature hamburger hors d'oeuvres right in her living room. She orders petit buns (2 inches in diameter) from her bakery and you should see the line queue to the right! A "Sunday" carpenter built a table with aged bricks over sterno heaters that keeps his informal buffet suppers warm, and then there's the young couple who found a mini wood-burning stove that looks adorable in their early American setting. This conversation piece is used frequently to keep popcorn, hot cider, chestnuts, etc., warm.

MARINADE FOR CUBED BEEF

For our Open House, we decided to marinate 1 1/2-inch cubed filets overnight and let our guests charcoal-broil them over our hibachi stove placed on our early American cobbler's bench.

People are still asking for our marinade recipe, but of course, we won't tell because I believe one should have a few specialties of the house. Besides they'd be disappointed if they knew our simple secret. All we did was buy a prepared Japanese sauce, Kikkoman Teriyaki marinade! (See Sources of Supply)

FLUFFY LIVER PATE

2 lbs. fresh chicken livers
1 medium-sized onion, chopped fine
3/4 cup salad dressing (Miracle Whip)
1 tablespoon brandy
1 hard-cooked egg, chopped fine
Salt and pepper to taste

1. Boil chicken livers in covered saucepan, medium heat, 10 to 15 minutes. Remove from heat, drain and cool. Chop livers finely and add finely chopped onions to liver.

2. Put in medium-size mixing bowl or electric mixer. Add salad dressing, brandy, chopped hard-cooked egg, salt and pepper. Either beat by hand for about 10 minutes, or until it is fluffy; or put in electric mixer at medium speed for 10 minutes or until fluffy.

3. Butter mold, fill with pate and place in refrigerator for several hours or overnight. Take out of refrigerator half hour before removing from mold. If necessary, place hot, wet towels on mold to help loosen pate. (There are attractive chicken-shaped molds on the market that are appropriate for chicken pate.)

RAINBOW OR BROOK TROUT

What bliss stuffing on fresh oysters at a New Orleans style oyster bar, or munching on San Francisco Bay crab, or savoring Maine lobster or gorging on Oregon salmon! In our part of the country, we specialize in smoked lake trout and whitefish, and no cocktail party is complete without this local delicacy.

But for a special treat we like to serve freshly caught rainbow or brook trout, which my husband catches in his private trout stream. He likes to poach the whole trout in homemade pickle juice and serve it cold as an hors d'oeuvre. We did a little experimenting and found we can achieve good results now using frozen trout and commercial pickle juice, which means we can serve this treat all year 'round.

> 2 pounds frozen trout
> 1 3/4 cup juice from a jar of Kosher dill pickles
> 1/4 cup vinegar*
> 6 cloves
> * Omit vinegar when using homemade pickle juice.

1. Preheat oven to 350°F. Place whole frozen trout, head and all, in a shallow pan uncovered and add liquid. After 15 minutes, when skin is tender, place 3 cloves through the skin of each fish. Baste occasionally. A large or 1 lb. frozen trout will be done in 40 to 50 minutes (fresh trout only takes about 10 to 15 minutes).

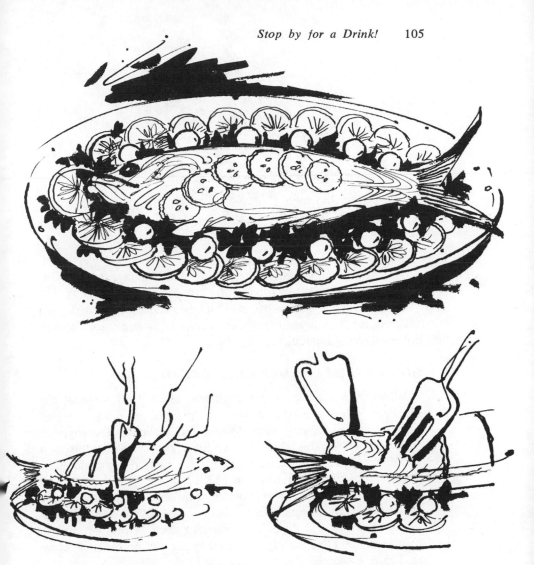

2. Cool and place fish whole on a platter and garnish with fresh parsley, chervil or watercress, and serve at room temperature.

Addenda: There's a bit of hocus-pocus connected with boning this delicacy which should be done before your guests. For this you'll need an extra bone plate.

1. With a sharp knife, sever the backbone vertically at head below gills and on tail section.

2. With a flat fish knife, or spatula, cut individual portions down to the backbone, but do not sever the backbone.

3. Lift the individual portions from the top layer of the fish and serve bits of fish on rounds of toast or crackers.

4. After the top layer has been served, the exposed backbone and ribs can be loosened easily and removed in one piece, leaving bottom layer for additional servings.

HOT CRABMEAT COCKTAIL SPREAD

When fresh seafood is not available, fill in with some of the excellent canned products on the market including canned sardines, clams, oysters, tuna, lobster and crabmeat. Usually, the best products of this kind are the most expensive but this is a variable matter. Do ask your friends for their recommendations if you haven't found brands you like.

An unusual canned hors d'oeuvre available at my fish market is frozen crab fingers. Serve them cold with a horseradish-mayonnaise dip and if you've never had them before, be sure to plan enough! (For the dip add a tablespoon of horseradish sauce to 1 cup mayonnaise.)

Supermarket freezers are well-stocked with herring in sour cream, frozen shrimp, lobster and crab. Shrimp, lobster and crab may be served cold with a dip or heated in bite-size chunks and served with a tangy sauce in a chafing dish. (A chafing .dish is nothing more than a double boiler that's crashed society).

8 ounces soft cream cheese
1 tablespoon milk
6 1/2 oz. drained, flaked crab meat

2 tablespoons finely chopped onion
1/2 teaspoon prepared horseradish
1/4 teaspoon salt
Dash of pepper
1/3 cup sliced toasted almonds

Combine cream cheese and milk. Add crabmeat, onion, horse-radish, salt and pepper. Blend well. Put in shallow ovenproof dish. Sprinkle with toasted almonds. Bake at 375°F. for 15 minutes. Serve with chips or crackers. Makes 1 1/2 cups.

When one thinks of fish foods, one should also think of ice because shrimp, caviar, lobster, crabmeat and oysters have greater eye-appeal when lavishly presented on shaved or chipped ice.

Your local tinsmith can easily make a container to fit on a teacart which can be wheeled anywhere indoors or out. Plates or shells of sea-food displayed on a sparkling layer of crushed ice with wedges of lemon and a choice of tangy dips is guaranteed to make the most sanguine guest raise a plucked eyebrow!

FRESH PINEAPPLE CHUNKS:

Refreshing fresh fruit of all kinds, but especially pineapple, I've found, is most welcome at cocktail parties. To improve the flavor of fresh pineapple chunks, boil 1/4 cup sugar with 1/2 cup water for 5 minutes and pour over chunks from one pine-apple. Let stand for 1 hour in sugar water. Optional: Soak pine-apple chunks in 1/4 cup Kirschwasser, (cherry brandy).

FRUITS IN LIQUEURS

The following liqueurs seem to go well with the accompanying fresh fruits as listed, but please don't feel these suggestions are binding. With a bit of experimenting you may discover your own special favorite combination. Of course fresh fruit and liqueur may be served at any time, either before or during a meal. When served as a dessert, add a scoop of sherbet.

Bourbon—peaches and pears
Brandy—strawberries, raspberries, peaches, pineapple
Champagne—peaches, berries, melons
Curaçao—oranges, pineapple, mandarin oranges
Grand Marnier—grapefruit, oranges, tangerines

Kirsch—bananas, cherries, melons, peaches, pineapple
Kummel—figs, peaches, pears
Port—raspberries, nectarines, melons, plums
Red Wine—peaches and strawberries
Rum—bananas
White Wine—apples, pears, purple plums

MORE ABOUT HORS D'OEUVRE:

The literal translation of the French word hors d'oeuvre is "outside of work" or something extraordinary or unusual. For years canapés and hors d'oeuvres made by professional chefs were elaborately garnished and beautifully designed jewel-like tidbits on which a great many hands spent a great many loving hours, but they usually didn't have much taste-appeal and, as time marched on, soaring costs and scarcity of labor, plus the fact that these fancies were no longer so extraordinary or unusual to sophisticated palates, forced a new trend in cocktail party hors d'oeuvres—simplicity. We fell unwilling heir to the dip, the devilled egg and the celery stuffed with cheese, but happily this day too is passing and today's trend seems the most sane development we've encountered in the evolution of the hors d'oeuvre. Today's popular hors d'oeuvres live up to their name—they're *extraordinarily* tasty because we've drawn *unusual* ideas from all over the world and developed them into our own inventive cuisine. Voila!

Ne-plus-ultra: Scoop out a little of the inside of a large, ripe strawberry and fill with black caviar and serve chilled.

CHINESE HARD-COOKED EGG

When I was a child I lived with my family in Shanghai, China for four years, where my father was in the import-export business. Like everyone else at that time, we had several in help including a Chinese cook named Fritz, who was an expert German cook. However he always prepared the staff meals "Chinese fashion" and one of my favorite treats when I wandered into the kitchen was a Chinees hard-cooked egg.

Today we serve the same egg as an hors d'oeuvre and it's just as popular on this side of the world because of its salty good flavor.

4 eggs
3 tablespoons soy bean sauce
1 tablespoon of Italian olive oil

Place eggs in pan and cover with cold water. Bring to a boil, reduce heat, and allow to cook about 15 minutes. Plunge the hard-cooked eggs in cold water for 5 minutes. Remove shells. In a small saucepan, heat soy sauce and olive oil, then place eggs in sauce, basting them until they become a light mahogany color. When cool, cut in quarters lengthwise with a sharp knife and serve—separately or as a garnish.

CAVIAR SAILBOATS

Sailing friends will be flattered when you salute them with this yachting hors d'oeuvre originated by Countess Henri de Vogue!

6 eggs
4 oz. jar of caviar
1 teaspoon lemon juice
1/2 teaspoon onion juice
12 toothpicks
12 strips of lemon or lime
1 bunch parsley

1. Place eggs in pan and cover with cold water, bring to a boil, reduce heat, and allow to cook about 15 minutes. Plunge the hard-cooked eggs in cold water for 5 minutes. Remove shells.

2. When cooled, cut in half lengthwise and remove yolk.

3. Fill center with caviar sprinkled with lemon and onion juice.

4. Press some egg yolk through sieve and sprinkle lightly over caviar.

5. Make a billowing sail by cutting lime or lemon rinds into 1/4-inch strips, and place toothpick through both ends, leaving one end of the toothpick longer than the other. Insert perpendicularly in egg for mast.

6. Place 12 sailboats on lush platter of parsley.

RAW VEGETABLE BOUQUET

It doesn't matter if your taste in art runs to contemporary action paintings or Old World still lifes, either way you'll have fun creating this arty centerpiece for your next summer cocktail table. It may add just the whimsical, pastoral touch you've been looking for.

Select a large white head of cauliflower. Cut a round hole in center, sink custard cup to be filled later with curry dip. Cut away about 2/3 of the buds intermittently in an even pattern. Place a toothpick in the vacancy and add carrot curls, radishes, miniature yellow and red tomatoes, raw cauliflower buds, bite-size pieces of zucchini, accenting some of the empty spaces with sprigs of fresh parsley or mint. Garnish the base of the cauliflower with large curly-leaf cabbage leaves. Serves 20 to 30 people.

CURRY DIP

1 cup mayonnaise
1 teaspoon Worcestershire sauce
1 tablespoon curry powder

In a small mixing bowl, mix mayonnaise, Worcestershire sauce, and curry powder until well blended. Refrigerate until ready to serve.

Addenda: There's a simpler, quicker and effective alternate presentation, on a lazy Susan, or on a round divided platter. Offer a variety of raw, tender, garden-fresh summer vegetables with a spicy curry dip placed in the center. Select vegetables when they are at their peak and arrange in alternate colors such as orange baby carrots next to buds of white raw cauliflower, green broccoli or snap beans, and red cherry tomatoes, beside strips of raw cucumbers, or tender green pea pods; or strips of yellow squash next to small stalks of white celery or rings of green pepper; and red radish flowers next to whole mushrooms.

RAW ONION TREES

Flank your vegetable bouquet with a pair of candles set in firm small cabbages or for a more sensational effect make a pair of edible onion trees. Here's how:

For two onion trees, buy 2 styrofoam cones about a foot high. Insert several dozen toothpicks into cone, then poke white spring

onions into picks starting at the top letting green stalks hang
down until cone is completely covered. Or, using the styrofoam
cones, one can build a *Strawberry Tree* with toothpicks. Everyone plucks his own berry and dips it in a saucer of powdered
sugar, whipped cream or sour cream.

MARINATED MUSHROOMS

    1 pound fresh mushrooms
    1 teaspoon salt
    3 tablespoons lemon juice
    1 cup vinegar
    1 bay leaf
    Pinch of freshly ground pepper
    Pinch of thyme
    2 shallots, cut fine
    1/2 cup olive oil
    1 tablespoon catsup
    1 tablespoon chopped chervil (optional)

Boil mushrooms for five minutes in salt water and lemon juice.
Drain water and dry mushrooms. In a small saucepan boil vinegar,
bay leaf, pepper, thyme, shallots for five minutes. Cool and add
olive oil, catsup and mushrooms. Marinate in refrigerator for at
least 3 hours. Before serving, strain dressing and pour back over
mushrooms. Sprinkle with fresh chervil if you have any in your
herb garden.

COLD ARTICHOKE LEAF DIP

When tender green artichokes are at their peak, cook and
remove leaves and arrange cold artichoke leaves on a round
platter. In the center, place a dip of mayonnaise (See recipe,
Mixed Dressing, Chapter II) to which add one tablespoon of
fresh horseradish. Or you might buy a prepared mayonnaise-with-
horseradish sauce instead. The leaves are picked up with fingers
and dipped one at a time in the sauce. The lower half of the leaf
is pulled between the teeth to extract the tender edible portion.
The leaf is then discarded on a separate plate.

How to cook an artichoke

Cut off stems and remove any tough bottom row of leaves. For 3 large or 6 small artichokes use 4 quarts of boiling water and add 3 tablespoons of salt and 2 tablespoons vinegar. Cook for 20 to 30 minutes, or until leaves pull out easily. Drain liquid. Remove leaves from center of "choke." Discard choke but reserve tender artichoke bottom, which is the most delicate part, to be used later as a salad with your favorite dressing. Serves about 20.

HOT POTATO BALLS

"What I say is that, if a man really likes potatoes, he must be a pretty decent sort of fellow."—A. A. Milne

Maybe this is the way some pretty important selections are made in Washington, D.C. these days for I'm told these hot potato balls are served at some of the most sophisticated parties there!

Make raw potato balls by using the same scoop-shaped knife one uses to make melon balls. Drop in boiling salt water to cover and cook until they are tender but still firm, about 8 or 10 minutes. Drain. Add melted butter and serve hot, hot on toothpicks. Figure two or three per person.

CANNED ARTICHOKE BOTTOMS

Artichoke bottoms (not hearts) are available in cans, usually 6 to 8 bottoms in each can. Serve cold. They are ideal used as vegetable casings filled with chopped broccoli or petit pois. See vegetables, Chapter VI.

Drain liquid and fill with prepared spread of Romanoff **Pate,** available in jars at any fine party store. May be topped with a dab of caviar.

Small size artichoke bottoms can be eaten as finger food, but large size bottoms are best served on a plate and eaten with **a fork.**

HOT CHUTNEY CRESCENTS

The dough for this Far East hors d'oeuvre is prepared the day before and refrigerated overnight. Or crescents may be made ahead and kept frozen.

1/2 cup butter
1 package (3 oz.) cream cheese
1 cup sifted flour
1/2 cup chutney

1. Start with butter and cream cheese at room temperature. In a medium size mixing bowl, cream together with a wooden spoon until smoothly blended. Add flour and mix thoroughly. Shape dough into a smooth ball, wrap in wax paper or aluminum foil and chill overnight in refrigerator.
2. Remove from refrigerator and let stand at room temperature for 1/2 hour. Roll dough to 1/8-inch thickness. Cut with 3-inch cookie cutter. Place 1 teaspoon of cut-up chutney in center of each round. Fold over and press edges together. Bake on ungreased baking sheet at 375° for 15 minutes. Serve warm. Makes 32 crescents.

Short Cut: Use Pillsbury Quick Crescent Dinner Rolls. Unroll 1 can dinner roll dough and proceed as above, cutting into 3 inch rounds. Makes 16 crescents.

CHUTNEY CHEESE HORS D'OEUVRE

For a quicker hot chutney hors d'oeuvre, try this recipe in your oven.

2 tablespoons butter
1 cup grated strong cheddar cheese
1/2 cup chutney
1/2 teaspoon dry mustard

Cream butter and cheese. Add chutney and mustard. Spread on toasted round of white bread. Bake on ungreased baking sheet at 450° for 5 minutes or until brown. Makes 4 dozen.

BLUE CHEESE WHEEL

Blue cheese is a popular hors d'oeuvre in Sweden where they serve a "wheel" with crackers. As an extra fillip, they scoop out the center of the wheel just a little and fill the well with the yolk of a raw egg. Guests mix cheese with egg yolk and spread the mixture on a cracker.

A superior blue cheese is processed in this country by the Maytag Dairy Farms in Iowa (See Sources of Supply). It is only available by mail, and they will ship 2 and 4 lb. wheels of blue cheese anywhere in the country along with a free cheese recipe booklet. This cheese keeps nicely in the freezer.

GARLIC TOAST HOT APPETIZERS

> 1/4 cup mayonnaise
> 1/2 cup chopped green onion, stem and all
> 1/2 lb. bacon bits
> 24 garlic rounds

In a small bowl mix mayonnaise, onions and bacon bits. Spread on toast rounds. Just before serving, put in 500°F. oven just long enough for spread to bubble. Makes 24 appetizers.

CELERY STUFFED WITH STEAK TARTARE

Cut individual pieces of celery into 3-inch strips and fill with Steak Tartare; see Chapter V for recipe.

SWEET 'N' SOUR COCKTAIL FRANKS

We've said it before—its not always what you serve but how you serve it that counts! This is true in the case of the humble hot dog which by any other name (Vienna Cocktail Frank) tastes just as sweet! Especially when cooked in the following sauce:

> 2 (5 oz.) cans Vienna Cocktail Franks
> 2 (10 oz.) jars currant jelly
> 1 (6 oz.) jar *French's* mustard

Simmer jelly and mustard for 2 hours. Add uncooked franks and continue cooking for another half hour. Transfer to chafing dish and serve bubbly hot with toothpicks.

GRILLED COCKTAIL WIENERS

Another amusing disguise for the pedestrian wiener is to serve either bite-size bits or miniatures on toothpicks placed in a leafy red or green cabbage. (To achieve a rose petal effect, core bottom of cabbage and roll outside cabbage leaves around a pencil toward center vein. Remove pencil and repeat.)

Cut a round hole in the center of the cabbage and insert a can of sterno. If you like, cover sterno with a sheet of copper screening. (For a smooth edge turn under about one inch.)

Marinate wieners in your favorite bar-b-que sauce and serve on toothpicks. Insert toothpicks in cabbage. Guests grill their own wieners over flames. Serve with Dijon mustard.

MINI-MEAT BALLS

These mini-meat balls are extremely flavorful, juicy and tender, and so easy to prepare in the oven in quantity before the party! Serve in a chafing dish.

    2 pounds fine ground round steak
    2 eggs
    3 slices whole wheat bread
    1 pound cottage cheese, small curd

1 cup yogurt
1 teaspoon M.S.G.
1 package dehydrated onion soup (Lipton's)
Dash of Beau Monde Seasoning
1 cup catsup

Preheat oven to 250°F. Combine everything but catsup; let stand for twenty minutes. Roll meat into small balls about the size of a very large olive. Place in a large shallow pan and bake in oven for one hour. Brown meatballs under broiler for five minutes turning once. Put in chafing dish and cover with thin layer of catsup and serve with toothpicks.

BOB'S BAR-B-QUED BEEFSTEAK

There probably aren't too many people around anymore who have had the pleasure of eating the piquant, juicy meat of an ox roasted in open pit, but if you ever have, it's a pleasure you never forget. There's only one slight drawback—it takes a half dozen strong men to dig the pit, rub the ox with salt and wrap him in parchment, muslin, etc. and serve the half a ton of bar-b-qued meat to a crowd of seven hundred people!

Thanks to Bob Neff of Charlevoix who's developed a recipe equally as delectable of more modest proportions, we're able to enjoy this flavorful hors d'oeuvre any time we're in the mood for a bar-b-que treat. His original recipe which he's never shared with anyone before is deceptively simple.

Order 6 dozen tiny hamburger buns (diameter 2 or 2 1/2 inches) from your bakery.

7 lbs. round steak cut 2 1/2 to 3 inches thick
1/4 cup salt
1 bottle (1 lb. 2 oz.) prepared Bar-b-que sauce

Rub salt into meat thoroughly. Place meat in a roaster with one quart of water. Cover and bake at 350°F for 3 1/2 hours. Remove from pan reserving liquid. With 2 kitchen forks, on a wooden cutting board shred meat into small pieces, mix shredded meat with most of the juice leaving 1/2 cup to add to chafing dish during the evening to prevent meat from becoming dry. Add bar-b-que sauce and stir until well mixed. Serve hot from chafing dish on warm hamburger buns.

HOT HORS D'OEUVRES WRAPPED IN BACON

One can't discuss hors d'oeuvres without mentioning this goody because it's so compatible with almost everything and may be prepared ahead then broiled in the oven at the last minute. And such variety!

Wrap any one of the following and secure with toothpicks. Broil in oven at 450°F. until bacon is crisp. (Timing varies depending on how lean or fat the bacon.)

1. Pineapple chunks
2. Large stuffed green olives
3. Sautéed chicken livers, plain or with water chestnuts
4. Prunes stuffed with almonds or walnuts, or chutney
5. Potato chip (requires no toothpick)

HORS D'OEUVRES ADDENDA

Refer to following chapters for hors d'oeuvre recipes:

Chapter III: Toasted Cheese Rolls, Toasted Mushroom Sandwiches, Stuffed Cherry Tomatoes, Hot Lobster Canapé, Merry-Go-Round Pie, Smoked Salmon.

Chapter V: Cheese Fondue, Baby Spareribs.
Beef Steak Tartare.

SAY "WHEN"

When it comes to the art of mixing drinks, there are several vocal but opposing schools of thought. Some people maintain the first drink should be good and strong—then go lightly on the rest. This misguided group claims after the first drink, nobody knows the difference! The tragic mistake in this approach is that when someone is tense, hungry and tired, a stiff drink can turn one into a drunk stiff! (Better coat the tummy, if you can, before the party, at home, with a cup of tomato juice or hot creamed soup.)

Another group suggests mixing all drinks equally strong; they rationalize the bartender is relieved from the chore of constantly refilling glasses. Then there's a third group who feel all drinks should be on the light side, keeping everyone drinking pleasantly and steadily all evening.

When you're playing bartender, the best advice is to use your own good judgment, and that includes pouring the "one for the road" back in the bottle when necessary. If you engage a professional bartender, don't hesitate to tell him how you'd like your drinks measured before the party starts. He'll be glad to follow your instructions.

HOW MANY FIFTHS

No matter how often one entertains, there's always the question, "How many bottles of liquor do we need?" Using the following measurements as a guide, one is able to judge the number of drinks per person.

> One case of liquor=twelve bottles
> 1/5 bottle=1/5 of a gallon, or 7 ounces less than a quart.
> 1/5 bottle liquor, using 1 ounce pony=25 drinks.
> 1/5 bottle liquor, using 1 1/2 ounce jigger=18 drinks.
> (The difference between a pony and a jigger is 1/2 an ounce.)
> 1/5 bottle champagne, using 3 ounce glasses=7 drinks.

The average guest will have two or three drinks, or figuring roughly one drink every 1/2 hour per person.

For a large group it's a good idea to use smaller glasses (6 or 8 oz.) because people frequently set a glass down and forget where they put it. For this reason, you'll need about 3 glasses per person.

Experts on alcoholism advise us against forcing drinks, and who isn't all for that! Better include some non-alcoholic beverages on your party list and give people who are dieting or who've sworn off alcohol a glass to hold without comment or apology.

Instead of an open bar, there are times it's preferable to pass trays of prepared or mixed drinks from the pantry or kitchen. Drinks can be mixed ahead and kept chilled in the refrigerator. Just add ice and garnish when ready to serve. For a large group you'll need some extra professional help, but for a small group, before dinner, the host can easily handle this job himself.

The sky's the limit when it comes to stocking a bar with a variety of wines and liquor, but the basic list includes only two whiskeys, Scotch and either rye or bourbon. (A rye man won't be offended when you offer him bourbon, or vice versa, but Scotch drinkers always like Scotch) Next on the list is Gin. Buy London gin at better prices, because cheap gin is for hangovers. Vermouth, vodka, sherry, and one or two after-dinner drinks round out the list.

BEFORE-DINNER WINES AND CHAMPAGNE

The study of wines is fascinating and connoisseurs have heaped much glamour and mystery on this subject. James Thurber, in one of his delightful cartoons, spoofs the self-styled critic, who is shown seated at the dinner table with his glass raised, saying, "It's a native, domestic Burgundy without any breeding, but I think you'll be amused by its presumption".

It's becoming more and more popular to serve a good grade of imported or domestic sherry (New York State grows wonderful grapes for sherries) or a Chablis (French white burgundy), or a fine California wine as a cocktail before dinner.

For festive occasions, such as wedding receptions or special anniversaries, imported champagne may be your first choice served pure, chilled and bubbly. A domestic champagne makes a good cocktail. (For Champagne punch, see Chapter III)

CHAMPAGNE COCKTAIL

Pre-chill champagne glasses and wine. Place a medium-size loaf of sugar in the glass and saturate with Angostura bitters— about 2 dashes. Fill glass with thoroughly chilled Champagne. Add a twist of lemon or orange peel.

AFTER-DINNER LIQUEURS AND CORDIALS:

"I thank you for your welcome which was cordial, and your cordial, which was welcome!"

More and more people are discovering the pleasant taste of an after-dinner cordial or liqueur, such as Crême de Menthe, Kahlua, Cointreau, Cherry Heering, etc. and I have just discovered George M. Tiddy's Canadian Liqueur which is brand new in the United States. This whiskey-based cordial is very smooth and not too sweet served straight from the bottle or, if you prefer, surprise your guests with a "Tiddy Bear."

TIDDY BEAR

1 part Tiddy's
1 part Vodka
1 wedge of lime or lemon

Serve in an old-fashioned glass over ice. That's all!

STEP-SAVERS:

When setting up an improvised bar indoors or out, drape a cloth around the edge of a large sturdy table, or aluminum folding table, that reaches all the way to the floor, behind which you can store extra liquor, lemons, limes, olives, napkins, glasses, soda water, ice buckets, empty bottles and a waste basket. In a small apartment a sturdy ironing board may serve as a bar if you're cramped for space.

Keep a large tray handy for quick trips to the kitchen with used glasses and figure using about three times as many glasses as there are guests.

BAR EQUIPMENT AND SUPPLIES

Some people tape a time-saving list inside the liquor closet door that may read something like this:

Liquor

Bourbon or Rye; Scotch; Gin, Vermouth; Sherry; Drambuie; Creme de menthe.

Soft Drinks

Cola drinks; Root beer; Ginger Ale.

Mixes

Soda Water; Quinine Water; Grape juice; Tomato juice.

Fruits, etc.

Lemons; Cherries; Olives; Onions.

Ice

Crushed, Cubed.

Supplies

Ice Bucket; Tongs; Bottle Opener; Corkscrew; Lemon Squeezer; Strainer; Water Pitcher; Long-handled bar spoon; Steel paring knife; Towel; Glasses; Coasters; Cocktail Shaker; Bottle Caps; Jiggers; Recipes.

A special word about ice. Ice bought at any metropolitan ice company is pure, whereas the ice from your own refrigerator may not be. Ice drinks up odors of a refrigerator as a sponge drinks up water.

INSTANT DRINK MIXES

What a convenience these new powdered instant mixes are for the yachtsman, vacationer, traveller or every woman who's infelicitous when caught suddenly in a bartending situation, when a request is made for anything more than a simple order of Scotch on the rocks!

All one needs for a good Whiskey Sour, a Tom Collins or a Mai Tai or almost any abracadabra one can think of in addition to the mix is liquor, ice and then shake well or better yet, put in a blender. It's a good idea to have a selection of powdered mixes on hand in your liquor closet just in case!

WHAT EVERY YOUNG BARTENDER SHOULD KNOW

There's a good story making the rounds at cocktail parties, so please stop me if you've heard this one!

A young Royal Mountie is having his gear checked by his instructor for his first solo into the hinterland. As they look over the gear, item by item, they come to the last small package.

"What's this?" inquires the Rookie.

"That's in case you get lost."

"But I have my compass."

"This is in case you *really* get lost, man," says the instructor, pointing to the contents of the package.

"Here's a small bottle of gin, and here's some vermouth, and here's a bottle of olives. Mix yourself a martnii and within two minutes someone will walk up to you and tell you that you didn't do it right!"

A RESPECTABLE MARTINI

Domestic Gin
Italian Dry Vermouth
Lemon Peel
Stuffed Olive or Onion

Pre-chill glasses and shaker and even the liquor if you're fussy.

Fill shaker with cubed ice and quickly pour three, four or five parts gin, depending on taste, to one part Italian (dry) Vermouth. Stir quickly, but gently. Promptly pour into cocktail glass. Rub lemon peel around edge of glass before serving. Add stuffed olive or onion.

BLOODY MARY

Mix one part vodka with two or three parts tomato juice, according to taste. Add a dash of Worcestershire sauce and a dash of lemon to taste. Salt and pepper, a dash of Tabasco sauce and ice complete the drink.

BULLSHOT

Three parts canned boullion to one part vodka and ice. No seasoning.

MARGARITA

The Margarita, a Mexican drink, is fast becoming a favorite summer drink throughout our country. It is made with tequila, and some brands are stronger than others so be careful. No ice is added to this drink and it is intended to be sipped very slowly from a cocktail glass frosted with salt! Yes, *salt*!

    1 1/2 oz. tequila
    1/2 oz. Triple Sec
    1 teaspoon fresh lemon or lime or 1/2 oz. unsweetened
       bottled lime juice

Wet glass and chill in freezer. If you like, rub edge of glass with lemon. Dip rim into a saucer of table salt and serve in 3 oz. or 3 1/2 oz. cocktail glass.

PINEAPPLE SWIPES

This ancient Hawaiian libation might be called the granddaddy of our packaged mixed drinks. All one needs for this novelty is a sun-ripened pineapple; slice off the top with a long-bladed knife, carefully cut up the interior without puncturing the outer skin, add a cup of sugar and a cake of yeast, replace the top and secure with toothpicks, let it set in the warm tropical sun for three lovely days. At the end of this time, uncap the pineapple and sit yourself in the cool shade of a coconut tree and sip the smooth tropical nectar. It won't be long before you'll hear the song of a nightingale!

What—you say? No sun-ripened pineapple? No coconut tree? Then try this short cut.

BEACHBOY SCREWDRIVER

    1   jigger vodka
    1/2 cup pineapple juice

Pour vodka over ice cubes in highball glass. Add pineapple juice. Garnish with orchid, azalea or gladioli blossom. For a frosted cocktail, mix in blender with ice for about 60 seconds at high speed.

BROKEN LEG

My favorite hot après-ski drink (originated by the Old Crow Distillery Co.) is called Broken Leg. It's easy to prepare, not too sweet and not too sour but so-o-o smooth!

For each portion allow:

6 oz. apple juice
1 stick cinnamon
1 thin slice lemon
1 oz. Bourbon, 80 proof

Heat apple juice. Place cinnamon, lemon slice and Bourbon in individual mugs. Add hot apple juice and enjoy, enjoy.

PLANTER'S PUNCH

1 teaspoon sugar
1/2 oz. orange juice
1 oz. lime juice
1 1/2 oz. dark rum
Soda water
Garnish: orange slice and a cherry

Dissolve sugar in fruit juices. Add rum. Shake and pour into highball glass filled with crushed ice. Add soda water and garnish with orange slice and cherry. Serve with straw.

TEN-DAY MINT JULEP

For years I was intrigued by pictures of herb gardens and recipes using herbs. I was fascinated by magazine articles describing in detail how to freeze them, dry them, and store them. I admired shiny bright photographs showing fresh herbs growing in neat little squares bordered by red brick walks or planted inside the spokes of an old wagon wheel.

But the closest thing I ever got to an herb was the dried jars on my grocer's shelves.

Though I longed to have a formal herb garden of my own, I was intimidated by these ancient aristocratic plants. Decorative herb charts threw me into a panic. Suppose I put the wrong herb in the stew? What would happen if I used too much marjoram or not enough basil?

It wasn't until a friend came along who knew all there was to know about herb gardening that I overcame my timidity. With her encouragement and advice, I plunged into this new culinary adventure with a vengeance. She readily convinced me that herb gardening was really quite simple. Growing mint and other herbs is no more complicated than growing any ordinary house plant, and it's so much more rewarding!

First, she helped me select the right spot in my garden. She chose a small triangular plot, not much bigger than a throw rug, next to the kitchen door. The area is sunny and the soil happens to be slightly acid as required.

With some old brick that was lying around in the back of the garage, we divided the plot into twelve sections. Next, we bought a basic selection of herbs from the local florist, a nearby super-market and a friendly farmer. We planted thyme, chives, mar-joram, basil, dill, chervil, and two kinds of mint—peppermint and curly leaf as a start. We placed the tall herbs such as dill and basil at the rear and the short ones such as thyme and chervil in the front. We still had a few squares left, so we decided to use one for parsley and another for cherry tomato plants, which our children love to pick.

Before too long, I began plucking tender young sprigs from the garden which I rinsed in the kitchen sink. Then carefully I removed the leaves from the stems because my friend cautioned me that stems have a bitter taste. While chopping herbs with one hand, I conscientiously balanced an herb chart in the other.

That first summer everything we ate was complimented with herbs! We had mint in our juleps, chives on our eggs, thyme in our stew, basil on our tomatoes, chervil on our fish, dill in our potato salad and marjoram in our soup.

The only thing served pure was milk!

Then one glorious day, I discovered a recipe using a variety of herbs mixed with butter and placed between thick slices of French bread. The whole thing is then wrapped in foil and heated in the oven. Delicious!

HERB BREAD

Bread
1/2 pound melted butter
1 teaspoon basil, chopped
1 teaspoon thyme, chopped
1/2 teaspoon marjoram, chopped

Cut Vienna or French bread into thick slices and spread over with herb butter and wrap in aluminum foil. Place in an oven preheated to 350°F for ten minutes. Serve in wicker basket.

By that time, even I had to admit I'd gone overboard on the herb bit. I pledged to myself that from then on I would only season one dish at a meal with herbs. And, happily, I've been able to stick to this sensible resolution. At this point, I also stopped referring to the chart incessantly and began using herbs indiscriminately in our cooking.

What's so great about herb cookery, one might ask? Well, it gives your tired old recipes a lift. It makes them taste new and special. The flavor of herbs themselves is hardly discernible. They're far more subtle than seasonings, such as salt, pepper, onions, mustard and catsup. People will rarely notice the flavor of thyme or marjoram, but they will notice your stews, gravies, salads and soups tasting extra good! And herbs make such a lovely garnish on platters, too.

TEN-DAY MINT JULEP

If it's true that the ancient Greeks and Romans called herbs the "wit" of cooking, then the barman who concocted the first Ten-Day Mint Julep must have been a very witty fellow, because this drink carries quite a punch!

1/2 cup sugar
2 jiggers brandy
Rye or Bourbon
Fresh mint sprigs, crushed

Pour sugar into quart mason jar. Tightly pack with tiny sprigs of fresh crushed mint until full. Add two jiggers of brandy, then fill to top with rye or bourbon. Do not stir, but keep jar refrigerated and invert the jar each day for 10 days. To serve, pour 2 ounces of mint concentrate over crushed ice. Garnish with fresh sprig of mint. Makes 1 quart.

FRESH MINT SAUCE

And speaking of mint, when Sir Walter Scott and his wife were taking a stroll in the meadows of Abbotsford, his country home, they stopped to admire a field where a herd of sheep were grazing. "It's no wonder", exclaimed Sir Walter, "that poets and philosophers have always made the lamb the emblem of peace and innocence."

"They are indeed delightful little creatures" agreed his wife, "especially with mint sauce."

   1 cup water
   1 cup vinegar
   2 cups sugar
   1 cup firmly packed mint leaves

In a medium-size saucepan, cook water, vinegar and sugar for 3 minutes, then add finely chopped firmly packed mint leaves. Remove from heat and let stand overnight. Strain and seal in hot sterilized jars.

THE FROZEN DAIQUIRI

A good daiquiri is made with good rum!

   1/2 teaspoon sugar
   1/4 teaspoon lime juice, fresh
   1 jigger light rum

Shake vigorously with plenty of finely crushed ice and strain into chilled cocktail glass. Or mix ice, sugar, lime juice and rum in blender. Garnish with sprig of mint.

Informal Cocktail Suppers

"Where there's room in the heart, there's room in the house."
—Danish Proverb

THE COCKTAIL SUPPER—
AMERICA'S CONTRIBUTION TO ENTERTAINING

A fun-loving couple from Cleveland sent out more than fifty cocktail-supper invitations in honor of their tenth wedding anniversary. They engaged a cateress and a couple of bartenders for the happy occasion, and as car after car pulled up in front of the circular driveway, guests were greeted by the welcome glow of flickering Hawaiian torches. At the entrance a white jacketed butler opened the door wide and lively music drifted across the bright threshold. As the smiling hostess greeted her guests, one of the ladies gushed, "Why honey—you fussed!"

Now it's no secret to anyone who cares about these things that giving a successful party does take a certain amount of fussing, and hosting an outstanding party is not an effortless, unplanned, unbudgeted, haphazard happening! It's work, but the synergistic kind of work that can be a delightful challenge, a satisfying experience and a world of fun.

FOUR SEASONS COCKTAIL SUPPER
BUFFET: FOR 16

The advantage in giving a cocktail supper rather than a sit-down dinner is that there is so little regimentation! Guests arrive early or late, drink as long as they like, eat when they're ready, sit down where they choose, leave when they wish, and the hostess couldn't care less.

Another advantage is that when people call the hostess to accept or decline an invitation, or procrastinate with "I'm not sure if we'll be in town on that date—we had better decline. May we have a raincheck?", she can honestly reply "We do want you to come—let us know when you can!" Or if someone says, "We can't be with you because we're having house guests from out-of-town", she can sincerely follow up with, "Please come and bring your friends!" (The Bible tells us, "Be not forgetful to entertain strangers, for thereby some have entertained angels unawares." Hebrews X III, 2.)

I do enjoy giving cocktail suppers, and mine usually start small and grow like Topsy! My husband still teases about the time I asked him if it would be okay to have a few people over for a drink on the 15th—and we ended up with 85 for a cocktail supper!

Before a party, I always prepare a written timetable along with the menu and tape this schedule on a kitchen cabinet for a last-minute check, both for myself and any extra help that's engaged for the party. On the check-list I write the number of guests, the time cocktails and hors d'oeuvre are to be served and when the hot things are to be put on the table, plus who's responsible for what.

When it's time to serve, the chafing dishes, platters and covered casseroles are set out on a long sideboard taking special care to keep food warm on electric hot trays. The following menu is an easy cocktail supper choice any time of the year because the spaghetti sauce can be prepared ahead or frozen as can the elegant Dobos Torte and Kumquat Bundt Kuchen.

Four Seasons Cocktail Buffet for 8 couples

Hors d'oeuvres (see Chapter IV)
Artichoke Leaf Dip
Brie Cheese   Blue Cheese Wheel
Beefsteak Tartare
with Rye Bread
Crabmeat and Oyster Casserole
Spaghetti with Chicken Livers
Brandy Cherry Ring
Dobos Torte   Kumquat Bundt Kuchen (see Chapter II)
Peppermint Candy
Mocha Coffee

BEEFSTEAK TARTARE

2 lbs. ground round steak
3 raw egg yolks
1/4 teaspoon Tabasco Sauce
1 tablespoon onion juice
1 tablespoon lemon juice
1 teaspoon Worcestershire sauce
Salt and pepper to taste
2 tins (2 oz. each) rolled anchovies
1 bottle pearl onions (4 oz.)
Parsley

1. Ask your butcher to remove fat from 2 lbs. of ground round steak and grind fine in clean meat grinder. He'll understand if you tell him you're going to eat the meat raw! (The color and flavor of round steak is at its peak when meat is freshly ground and served.)

2. Mix well with three raw egg yolks. Season with Tabasco sauce, onion juice, lemon juice, Worcestershire sauce, salt and pepper; mix well.

3. Put in a pretty mold and let it stand for an hour or so in refrigerator before removing it to a platter. Garnish with rolled anchovies and pearl onions and a little parsley. Makes 16 servings.

Addenda: Steak Tartare is also good as an hors d'oeuvre or luncheon dish for men. Season meat. Shape it as you would a hamburger patty. Make indentation in center for raw egg yolk, garnish with anchovies and pearl onion, and parsley. Serve with triangles of toast. Makes 8 servings.

CRABMEAT AND OYSTER CASSEROLE FOR 16

2 qts. fresh or frozen oysters
1 onion grated
2 tablespoons green pepper chopped medium
1/4 cup butter
4 tablespoons flour
Cream, salt
2 tablespoons lemon juice
1 teaspoon Beau Monde Seasoning (Spice Islands)
2 lbs. fresh or frozen crabmeat
1 cup bread crumbs

1. In a large saucepan, cook oysters in their own liquid until edges curl.

2. In the meantime sauté onion and green pepper lightly in butter in a large skillet.

3. Add flour, oyster liquid and a little cream to thicken sauce. Stir.

4. Season with salt, lemon juice and Beau Monde Seasoning.

5. Add oysters and crabmeat.

6. Put all ingredients in a large uncovered casserole and sprinkle with buttered bread crumbs and bake in 375° F. oven for 40 minutes.

Addenda: This can be prepared in the morning but omit bread crumbs until reheating just before serving.

SPAGHETTI WITH CHICKEN LIVERS

1/2 cup dried mushrooms
2 cups soup stock or consommé
1 cup olive oil
2 large onions, chopped
2 green peppers, chopped
1 clove garlic, pressed or dash of garlic powder
1 can (1 lb.) Italian spaghetti sauce
1 can (1 lb.) tomatoes
1/2 teaspoon salt
1 teaspoon oregano
2 pounds spaghetti
1 pound fresh chicken livers
1/2 pound fresh mushrooms
6 slices Mozzarella cheese
2 teaspoon sugar
Dash of cayenne pepper

Sauce:

Sauce may be prepared in advance and frozen. Soak dried mushrooms for several hours in soup stock or canned consommé. Heat oil in a large iron skillet; brown chopped onions, peppers and garlic; simmer slowly for ten minutes. Add Italian spaghetti sauce, tomatoes, soup stock and dried mushrooms. Cook slowly covered for two hours.

Spaghetti:

On the day of the party, bring two large kettles of water to boil; add salt, oregano, then spaghetti; let cook for fifteen minutes, or until spaghetti is done *al dente* (firm but tender). Meanwhile sauté fresh chicken livers and mushrooms in butter. Drain spaghetti and mix with sauce and chicken livers, then season with sugar, cayenne pepper and put in a large casserole. Now cover with slices of Mozzarella Cheese. When ready to serve, heat in over 400°F. until cheese melts. Makes 16 servings.

BRANDY CHERRY RING

    1 can brandied Bing cherries
    1/2 cup walnut halves
    2 cups orange juice
    1 1/2 cup sherry wine
    1 cup sugar
    3 tablespoons gelatin

Dressing

    1/2 cup mayonnaise
    1/2 cup whipped cream

Drain cherries saving the juice; stuff them with nut meats. Combine the juice from cherries with 1 1/2 cups of orange juice (the other 1/2 cup is used later), wine and sugar, and bring to a boil. Now soak gelatin in remaining 1/2 cup orange juice then add to hot fruit syrup. When the mixture begins to set, put into a ring mold with cherries and nuts. Serve gelatin mold with mixture of mayonnaise and whipped cream set in a round dish in the center of the ring. Makes 16 servings.

DOBOS TORTE

The ingredients for making a Dobos Torte are so economical compared to the prices charged by professional bakers, and the results are so spectacular, it's hard to understand why more budget-minded gals don't make this *ne plus ultra* dessert. One of the nice things about making a Dobos Torte is that it can be done in two stages the day before. I usually bake the individual layers in the morning and make the chocolate icing in the evening, when things have quieted down around the house. The Torte freezes beautifully and is ready to serve whenever the spirit moves you. Just allow the usual defrosting time.

To make a Dobos Torte you need two, three, or four 8" spring form pans (with removable bottoms). It's speedier with several pans. The following recipe using 8" pans makes 6 layers. If you double the recipe you can add more layers and/or use 9- or 10-inch pans. There's just one thing, don't use pans of different sizes or your torte will droop on the sides when you put it all together. Another point, have all ingredients at room temperature.

Dough

    1 cup flour
    7 eggs, separated
    1/2 teaspoon salt
    1 cup powdered sugar

1. Preheat oven to 375° F. Put two sheets of wax paper on counter. Sift presifted flour once on wax paper, measure, then sift again four times.

2. In a large bowl beat egg yolks, salt and sugar until thick.

3. In another large bowl, beat egg whites stiff but not dry.

4. Alternately fold in flour and egg whites with egg yolk mixture lightly until smooth but still fluffy.

5. Butter and flour only the bottoms of the cake pans.

6. With a rubber spatula spread dough evenly on cake pan

about 1/4 inch thick. Bake in moderate oven from six to eight minutes. Dough should not turn brown but remain very pale yellow.

7. Remove cake at once from pan with a metal spatula and let cool. Repeat until all the dough is used. You should have 6 layers.

Filling and Icing

1/4 lb. sweet chocolate
1/4 lb. bitter chocolate
3 tablespoons water
3 eggs
1 1/2 cups powdered sugar
1/2 lb. butter
1 teaspoon vanilla

1. Melt chocolates with water in double boiler.
2. In a medium-size bowl, mix eggs and sugar and add to chocolate. Stir constantly until thick. This takes quite a while.
3. Remove chocolate mixture from stove. While it is cooling, cream butter until light. Add vanilla to butter, then add chocolate mixture and beat until well blended.
4. Spread a thin layer of chocolate mixture on cake, place another layer of cake on chocolate mixture and repeat until cake is 6 layers high, leaving enough chocolate to cover both top and sides of cake. Caution: Be sure to place layers very evenly one on top of the other. Allow torte to set a day before serving.

Addenda: A Dobos Torte is always sliced thin because it is quite rich. Makes 12 servings.

SUNDAY SUPPERS

The rosy afterglow of a Sunday evening get-together helps most people drive away those Monday blues. Young people, old people, in fact most people enjoy going to someone's home for a "gemütlich" Sunday evening supper. Since Sunday is such a relaxed, informal kind of play-day, it's a perfect time for single men and women to entertain family, friends or other single men and women. It's the one day of the week when almost anything goes! One can invite a medley of ages, teen-agers and parents;

one can invite more men than women or more women than men; one can arrange word games for young and old after dinner; one can sing songs or play the guitar; one can play bingo or bridge; one can show travel movies or spin old collectors disks; one can roast skish-ka-bob or pop-corn; one can play truth or consequences; one can play charades or backgammon or monopoly or hearts; one can dress up or down; one can have a lot of fun just being together with friends!

A friend who lives alone and likes it frequently entertains on Sundays because she's discovered a Sunday supper invitation is accepted joyously and enthusiastically. Sunday may be a trying day for people who live alone or for couples whose grown children have moved away to college campuses, army bases, or suburbia. Once there weren't enough minutes in the day for doing all the things that a family tries to squeeze into those precious twenty-four hours of togetherness; now the hours drag and one can't wait for the stimulation of a work week.

My single friend entertains with a flair. Though her menus are always carefully budgeted, they're still imaginative. We all look forward to her little Sunday night suppers because as she puts it, "I don't try to compete with fancy French restaurant food. My women friends feel it's a treat to enjoy some good home cooking in company—a meal they haven't had to plan or shop for." And the men love it because, "I always try to give them something hearty." She gives more than that.

Besides good food, there's always good discussion after dinner at her house, too. People one has known for years without ever exchanging more than superficialities suddenly become interesting and loquacious story tellers. How is this wonder accomplished? For one thing she serves a buffet, then sets up three card tables in her compact living room and after dinner she allows her guests to remain seated around the card tables for relaxed after-dinner cigars, brandy and light conversation.

"It's so much more comfortable this way for small group discussions. Sometimes people push a chair back and chat with the group at the next table, then break up into two's and three's again. I've found that when I remove the bridge tables and chairs, everyone ends up sitting around the living room in a large circle; and people become inhibited and have little to say."

When Boswell complained to his friend, Dr. Samuel Johnson "of having dined at a splendid table without hearing one sentence of conversation worthy of being remembered," Boswell replied

"Sir, there seldom is any such conversation!"

"Why then meet at the table?" Boswell asked.

"Why, to eat and drink together and to promote kindness; and, Sir, this is better done when there is no solid conversation; for when there is, people differ in opinion, and get into bad humour, or some of the company who are not capable of such conversation are left out and feel themselves uneasy."

Things haven't changed that much since 1776!

SUNDAY SUPPER WITH A GREEN THEME

The theme for the table decoration reflects the menu. An arrangement of bells of Ireland accented with green zinnias is flanked by a pair of candles placed in clear glass hurricane chimney holders. Rough earthenware crockery bowls and platters are set on a pale blue denim tablecloth.

Bells of Ireland Menu

Appetizers

Green Olives   Dilli-Beans
Hot Buttered Potato Balls (Chapter IV)
Senegalese Soup or Hungarian Green Noodles and
Cabbage Casserole
Corn Beef on Saddle of Rye Bread
Horseradish Sauce
Cucumber Salad   Pickles
Beer   Coffee
Boston Cream Cake

SENEGALESE SOUP

This smooth, delicate soup may be served hot or cold. It can be quickly assembled because the chicken broth can be prepared a day or even several days ahead.

    2 stalks finely chopped white celery
    1 large sliced onion
    3 medium sliced fresh apples
    1 banana (optional)
    1/2 lb. butter
    1/4 cup curry powder
    1/3 cup flour
    8 cups chicken broth (broth from one stewing
        chicken—see index for Soup Stock recipe)
    1/4 teaspoon salt
    1/4 teaspoon white pepper
    Dash of cayenne pepper
    2 cups light cream
    1/2 cup white wine

Sauté celery, onions, apples, banana in butter in a saucepan or skillet. Strain mixture through sieve into large saucepan. Add curry powder, blend in flour gradually. Add chicken broth and dry seasonings. Reduce heat and add cream. Do not allow to boil. Just before serving, add wine. Makes 10-12 servings.
Addenda: Pieces of diced white meat of chicken or chutney are sometimes served on the side.

HUNGARIAN GREEN NOODLES AND
CABBAGE CASSEROLE

I'll admit this sounds ordinary, but through alchemy the combination of these two standbys complement each other in such a way that an unusual party dish results.

    1 medium-size cabbage
    2 oz. butter or 4 strips of bacon
    1 medium size onion
    1 teaspoon salt
    2 small apples
    3 tablespoons red wine
    1 package (16 oz.) broad egg noodles

Slice cabbage medium fine. Rinse raw sliced cabbage with hot water through colander. Melt butter or bacon strips in a large frying pan. Slice onion very fine and sauté in frying pan until lightly brown. Add rinsed cabbage and simmer for 5 minutes. Add salt. Peel and quarter apples, add them to cabbage and simmer for 15 minutes. Cover frying pan and simmer for another 15 minutes. Add 3 tablespoons of red wine and simmer for 5 minutes. Before serving, cook noodles in boiling water as directed on package. Drain. Combine with cabbage and serve hot. Makes 12 servings.

FRESH CORNED BEEF ON RYE

Buy two fat (not lean) corned beef briskets totaling about 7 pounds; remove any cellophane. If your local butcher or delicatessen cannot supply first-rate quality, do not hesitate to send away for them; store them in your freezer until needed and defrost before using. Gunsberg Brisket packaged in Detroit is one of several superior brands.

    2 corned briskets of beef
    2 unsliced rye breads
    1/4 lb. butter (4 oz.) butter or margarine

Tie briskets separately with twine lengthwise very tightly and knot securely. Then tie each brisket crosswise twice. This holds the meat firmly together for carving. Place in one large pot or two medium-size pots and cover with cold water. Bring water to a rolling boil. Reduce heat and let simmer slowly for 3-1/2 to 4 hours or until meat is tender. Remove from water and place in shallow pan in warm oven for 15 minutes. When ready to serve, cut and remove twine. Cut off top, bottom and side crust from rye breads. Melt butter in frying pan and sauté bread on both sides. Place warm bread on serving platter and place corn beef on top of rye bread. When carving serve each person a slice of corn beef with a slice of rye. The juices of the meat flavors the bread. Garnish with parsley and be prepared to serve seconds! Makes 12-14 servings.

BOSTON CREAM CAKE

    4 eggs
    1 cup sugar

4 tablespoons hot water
1 cup flour
1 teaspoon baking powder
1/8 teaspoon salt
1 teaspoon vanilla
1 lemon rind, grated

Preheat oven to 350° F. Separate eggs. Beat egg yolks in a large mixing bowl, add sugar and continue mixing until thick and lemon colored. Add water. Sift flour and baking powder, salt and add to egg yolks. Beat egg whites until stiff and add vanilla and grated lemon rind. Bake in oven for twenty minutes.

Custard Filling

3 egg yolks
2 tablespoons flour
1 tablespoon cornstarch
1/2 cup powdered sugar
2 cups half and half cream
2 tablespoons butter
1 teaspoon vanilla
1 cup whipped cream

Cook everything except whipped cream in double boiler, stirring occasionally until thick. Cool. Fold in whipped cream. Cut the two layers in half horizontally and spread with custard filling. Sprinkle top with powdered sugar or cover with chocolate frosting.

Chocolate Frosting

1/4 cup brown sugar
1/4 cup water
1 tablespoon butter
1 square bitter chocolate
1 cup powdered sugar
1/2 teaspoon vanilla

Boil brown sugar, water and butter; while stirring add chocolate. When melted, remove from range. Add powdered sugar, and vanilla; beat with egg beater until smooth. Makes 10 servings.

APRES-SKI PARTY (AND OTHER IMPROMPTU GET-TOGETHERS)

One of the most delightful "happenings" occurs when people join you at the spur-of-the-moment for potluck meals.

Does the thought of company for potluck appall you? It certainly will if you maintain that the whole house has to be spic-and-span—but if hanging out a fresh guest towel will do, then you'll have all the time and energy needed to enjoy the companionship of people.

Living in a summer and winter resort as we do, unexpected company (that doesn't mean *unwelcome* company!) is almost a weekly occurrence. Admittedly there are times one wishes one could repeat the "miracle of the loaves" (unhappily no one can tell us how to make two pork chops into four), but there are ways of stretching dinner by adding an extra course, opening an extra can or defrosting an extra cut of meat.

During ski season we often meet friends on the slopes and invite them home for potluck; this usually means charcoaling hamburgers or steaks in our own fireplace. For this we use a device called a swinging grill, a simple attachment composed of a fixed pole that fits into the grate, opening vertically, to which a grill is hooked that can be raised or lowered at will. (See Sources of Supply) The taste of meat charcoaled over a wood fire is very special, however if one does not have a fireplace, there's always the option of grilling the conventional way on a smokeless charcoal burner or in the oven.

The first thing we do when we return home, before we even remove our boots, is to light the grate fire so that by the time our guests arrive the logs have burned down to bright hot embers. Next, out comes the meat from the deep-freeze along with a homemade Bundt Cake and a loaf of sourdough bread. We quickly spread a bright green cloth on our dining-room table for our buffet and arrange the silverware and napkins for self-service. Our large soup tureen is placed at one end of the table to be filled with Crab-Bisque—a hot, filling soup that really hits the spot after a salubrious day on the snow—or in the snow, as the case may be!

While we're bathing and changing into comfortable after-ski outfits, our dinner is defrosting. Soon the doorbell starts ringing and everyone gathers around the fire, sipping soup, while the inevitable kibitzer has his fun directing the precise grilling of his steak—how raw is rare; how pink is medium? After the hot soup course, warm plates are set out, along with some good homemade relishes and warm bread, sliced thick and served in straw baskets. Our simple menu is quite filling even without vegetables or potatoes, but if one is lucky enough to have a potato casserole of Cheese Magic in the freezer—this apres-ski menu will guarantee a standing ovation!

Finally, with either a cold beer or a chilled glass of rosé wine in hand, it's time to recount tall tales of thrills, chills and spills on the various slopes.

Apres-Ski Potluck

Cocktail—Broken Leg (chapter IV)
Hors d'oeuvre: Saratoga Chips wrapped in bacon
or
Crab Bisque and Crackers
Homemade Corn Relish, Pickles, Olives, Carrots,
Celery Sticks
Charcoaled Grilled Steak
Sourdough Bread (bought)
Cheese Magic
Imported Beer
Bundt Cake (see chapter II)
Rosé Wine
Cafe Royal

CRAB BISQUE

1 can 10 1/2 oz. condensed tomato soup
1 can 10 1/2 oz. creamed pea soup
2 cans 10 1/2 oz. each, milk
1 can (7 oz.) crab meat
1 tablespoon Sherry
1 pint whipped cream topping
(low calorie)

Mix soups and milk in large double boiler and bring to boil. Drain crab meat and remove bones and add to soup. Just before serving pour in a tablespoon sherry. Warm soup tureen and soup plates in oven. When ready to serve pour hot soup in tureen and serve with in individual soup plates, topped with whipped cream topping. Makes 6 servings.

HOMEMADE CORN RELISH

(keeps a long time in the refrigerator.)
1 can (12 oz.) whole kernel corn
1 teaspoon mustard seed
1/2 teaspoon dry mustard
1/4 teaspoon salt
1/4 teaspoon pepper
1/3 cup cider vinegar
1 tablespoon salad oil
2 tablespoons light brown sugar
1/2 cup chopped onion
2 canned pimientos, drained and chopped
1/4 cup chopped green pepper

Drain liquid from corn into small saucepan. Stir in mustard seed, mustard, salt, pepper, vinegar, oil and brown sugar. Bring to a full boil. Mix together corn, onion, pimiento, and green pepper in medium bowl. Pour hot liquid over corn mixture. Toss lightly until well mixed. Refrigerate covered several hours before serving. Makes 2 1/2 cups.

CHEESE MAGIC

Not a souffle—not a pudding—but a kind of magical delight that brings rave revues from the critics. Make it the day before or freeze it for any performance.

8 slices white bread, buttered
1/4 lb. butter for casserole
1 1/2 lbs. sharp cheddar cheese, grated
6 eggs
1 finely minced green onion
1/2 teaspoon dry mustard
1/2 teaspoon Beau Monde
seasoning (Spice Island)

1/2 teaspoon salt
1/4 teaspoon paprika
1/8 teaspoon cracked black pepper
Dash of cayenne
2 1/2 cups half-and-half cream
1 rounded teaspoon brown sugar
1/2 teaspoon Worcestershire sauce

Remove crust from bread and butter well. Dice into about 1/4-inch squares. Generously butter 2-quart casserole, arrange bread on bottom, lay generous layer of grated cheese on top, then more bread and second half of remaining cheese. Beat eggs and add green onions, dry seasonings, half-and-half, then brown sugar and Worcestershire sauce. Pour over bread and let stand 24 hours in refrigerator. Two hours before baking remove from refrigerator and let stand at room temperature. Preheat oven to 300°F. Set casserole in a shallow pan of water with heavy paper on bottom. Bake for 1 1/2 hours. Makes 12 servings.

CAFE ROYAL

After the last sigh, "I'm so full!" and while everyone is still languishing before the fire, it's time to nudge the group gently by offering them a flaming surprise. For this witchery, turn the lights low, bring in a tray with a pot of hot strong coffee, cups, saucers and some fine brandy along with a dish of cubed sugar for Cafe Royal.

We use brandy burning spoons that hook over the rim of a cup (See Sources of Supply), but you can easily do without

them if you have a steady hand. Just be sure to warm the spoon first by holding it over the hot coffee for about a half a minute, then place a cube of sugar in the spoon, add a little brandy and ask one of the gentlemen to light the brandy with a match for you. As the brandy flames, lower the spoon gently into the coffee just below the surface. This will ignite the surface of the coffee. Swish the spoon gently back and forth in the cup until the flame dies out. An added twist of lemon is optional.

THE BACK-YARD BARBECUE

This little rhyme was composed by Felix Jewell, a jewel of a professional chef whose back-yard barbecues were never like the one he describes:

The charcoal smoked
The steak was burned
The corn was raw
The host concerned
The meal was late
The children whined
Mosquitoes swarmed
And amply dined
The night was cold
The moon obscured
And, I the guest
Was bar-b-*cured!*

Cooking outdoors can be a delight or disaster! Little things like a shift in the prevailing wind can fill the garden with smoke instead of sunshine. A broiling sun can melt the chilled consommé, because, contrary to general opinion, jellied dishes are not good for summer buffets unless they are kept chilled over ice. Aromatic good food can attract a horde of insects (but spraying the party area with a good insecticide seems to take care of that problem, and I find that local hardware people always know the brands that work best on local pests).

The following menu is one of my favorites.

My Favorite Barbecue Menu

Mint Juleps
Merry-Go-Round Pie (see Chapter III)
Barbecued Chicken
Cole Slaw
Tomato Pudding Red-Fox or Puree   Corn on the Cob
(in boiling water needs less than 5 minutes!)
Dilli Casserole Bread
Cheese Pie with Fresh Strawberries
Coffee

BARBECUED CHICKEN TIMED TO PERFECTION

Perhaps the biggest bugaboo in barbecuing is timing. I learned the hard way, when grilling chicken, that either my chicken or my guests suffered (and one always led to the other!). Sometimes the broilers were still raw when we were ready to eat, other times perhaps we dallied over cocktails and the chickens were overdone. Here's a recipe that never misses!

Marinate broilers or small frying chickens in your favorite Italian dressing; let stand in shallow pan several hours. Drain. Place in a low preheated oven (325°F.) uncovered and precook for about 45 minutes. Light charcoal fire. About 15 minutes before you are ready to eat, brown the chickens over the charcoal grill and paint with melted butter several times while turning.

TOMATO PUDDING RED FOX

There's a remarkable eating place in what is now affectionately called "Hemingway Country" in Northern Michigan. Red Fox Inn is the scene of one of Ernest Hemingway's earliest short stories; shouting distance down the road is a little white frame church where he was first married. Any stranger driving by the

Red Fox Inn would never notice that simple white farmhouse because there are no gay signs endorsing its excellence. But the *cogniscenti* arrive by jet and Lincoln Continental on a nostalgic pilgrimage from far-off New York, Chicago and New Orleans to savor Fox's country-fresh chicken dinners with dumplings and gravy, freshly picked tender young corn on the cob, crisp cole slaw salad, hot cheese rolls, homemade pickle relish, and strawberry jam.

How many family birthdays and anniversaries we've celebrated in the same original and unpretentious setting! How many times we've walked up the uneven painted steps to wait on the narrow screen porch with the slanting floor where one can have a drink before dinner—if you bring your own liquor! And how many discussions have been waged as to who's best able to duplicate the tomato pudding. There are those who say it's best made with tomato purée—and Mrs. Dwight Eisenhower belongs to this school. Not only did Mrs. Eisenhower frequently serve the President's favorite dish during their term in the White House, but in a letter to me she recalls the first time she tasted it—at Mrs. George Humphrey's plantation in Georgia. Good recipes travel far!

An equally staunch group of gourmets maintain that tomato pudding is best prepared with whole tomatoes because the presence of seeds adds to the flavor and texture of the pudding.

Fortunately, I possess the original recipe as given to Mrs. Fox by a former summer visitor. It can be prepared in two stages, and also in the quicker puréed version. Which recipe do you like best? The proof of the pudding lies in the eating!

>   1 can (12 oz.) cooked tomatoes
>   1/2 cup dark brown sugar (packed)
>   1/4 cup melted butter
>   1/4 teaspoon salt
>   1 cup dry white bread cut into 1 inch squares
>   1/3 cup bread crumbs

Drain tomatoes. Add sugar, butter, salt, dry bread. Cook slowly on top of stove for two and a half hours. Remove from stove and put in baking dish. Sprinkle with bread crumbs and bake uncovered for 30 minutes at 375°F. Makes 8 servings.

TOMATO PUDDING PUREE

   1 10-oz. can tomato purée
   1 cup dark brown sugar
   1/4 teaspoon salt
   1 cup fresh white bread cut into 1-inch squares
   1/2 cup melted butter

To purée add sugar and salt, heat to boil, and reduce to simmer for 5 minutes. Place bread squares in casserole and pour melted butter over bread. Add hot tomato mixture and bake covered for 30 minutes in moderate oven at 375°F. Makes 8 servings.

DILLI CASSEROLE BREAD

   1 pkg. active dry yeast or 1 cake compressed yeast
   1/4 cup warm water
   1 cup creamed cottage cheese heated to lukewarm
   2 tablespoons sugar
   2 tablespoons finely chopped onion
   1 tablespoon butter
   2 tablespoons dill seed
Dash of salt
   1/4 teaspoon baking soda
   1 unbeaten egg
   2 1/4 to 2 1/2 cups sifted flour
   1 teaspoon lemon pepper (Optional)

Soften yeast in water. Combine in a large mixing bowl warm cottage cheese, sugar, onion, butter, seed, salt, soda, egg and softened yeast. Slowly add flour to form a stiff dough, beating well after each addition. Cover, let rise until double in size, about 50 to 60 minutes. With a rubber spatula gently transfer dough into well-greased 8″ round oven-proof baking dish. Let rise again in well warmed place until light, 30 to 50 minutes. Preheat oven to 350°F. Bake for 40 to 50 minutes, until golden brown. Let dilli bread cool slowly in warm oven with door open. Brush with soft butter and sprinkle with lemon pepper. Serve warm. (Freezes well.) Makes 12 servings.

CHEESE PIE

There are cheese cake recipes and cheese pie recipes and you may have your favorite—but this one is mine! Why? One reason is because the very first time I tried it—perfection! We always make this in a 9" pie pan, the day before we plan to serve it. I do not recommend freezing. It's good served with fresh strawberries in the summer or maraschino cherry sauce in the winter.

Crust

> 18 graham crackers
> 1 tablespoon sugar
> 3/4 stick butter (scant 1/2 cup)

Roll crackers to crumbs with rolling pin. Place in medium-size bowl and add sugar. Melt butter in saucepan. Add melted butter to crumbs; press mixture against bottom and sides of pie pan.

Filling

> 1 lb. cottage cheese
>   (put through colander)
> 2 eggs
> 1/2 cup sugar
> 1/2 teaspoon vanilla
> Dash cinnamon

Press cheese through colander into medium-size bowl. In another bowl, beat eggs. Add to cheese with sugar, vanilla and cinnamon. Mix well, then transfer to lined pie pan. Place in preheated 375°F. oven for 20 minutes, then increase the temperature to 475°F., and add topping.

Topping

> 1 pint sour cream
> 2 teaspoons sugar
> 1/2 teaspoon vanilla

Mix together sour cream, sugar and vanilla, and pour over the baked mixture; return to 475°F. oven for five minutes. Cool, then chill. Serve with fresh berries. Makes 12 servings.

MAINLAND LUAU

One of the most unusual parties I ever attended was given in August by a bachelor whose tiny summer cottage is no larger than a four-room apartment. It opens up through sliding doors into a charming well-cared-for garden completely enclosed by a six-foot fence, giving one a feeling of great intimacy and complete privacy.

On this balmy summer evening, tall hurricane lights flickered among the shrubs and, as if by signal, a silvery moon rose over the bay. Bob had set up two folding tables for ten with folding chairs outdoors. The tables were covered with red and white checkered tablecloths. We noticed some activity in the corner and when we strolled over to inquire, we saw an enormous pit, approximately three feet wide, six feet long, and two feet deep, aglow with several layers of charcoal. Across the pit was a heavy metal mesh on which was stretched half a young pig, sizzling merrily. Well, this certainly wasn't going to be an ordinary dinner, though we should have known from the unusual invitation we received made from a scrap of leather with the wording pricked by needle!

In the dusk of the evening we noticed in another corner of the garden three saplings, braced and tied together at the top, from which an enormous black kettle was suspended by a long metal chain. Under the kettle a brisk fire was burning, but before we could wonder, Bob's housekeeper, an American Indian, approached us in full regalia—beads, feathers, deerskin dress and moccasins, carrying a huge basket of freshly picked corn. Into the kettle of boiling water went the corn and the lovely aroma made our mouths water. But not for long, because soon we were handed a plate and guided to a buffet table. Here the salad bar was a picture—a gastronomical delight.

First there was a large bowl of crisp, fresh, iceberg lettuce and another bowl of curly endive, accompanied by smaller bowls of sliced tomato and onion rings, sliced eggs, watercress, chopped celery, chopped green peppers, sliced cucumbers, sliced avocado, radishes and pickles, and a handsome pitcher of herb salad dressing. What fun we had concocting the salad of our choice!

I don't know if I'll ever get around to the roast pig with the Indian maiden, but what a grand idea this salad bar is for a

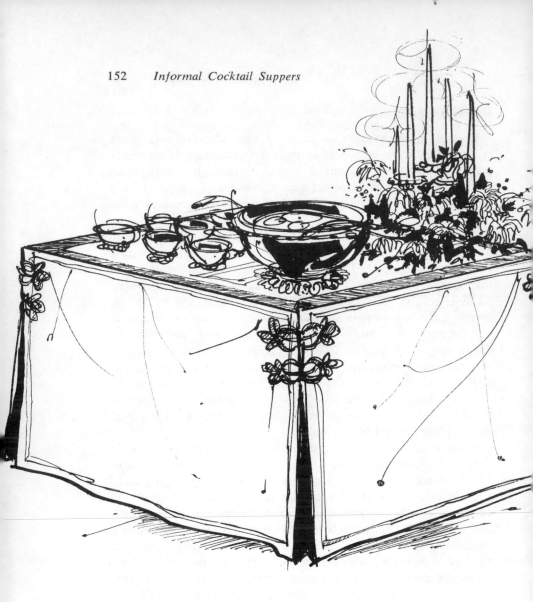

summer luncheon. My economical heart jumped with joy when I realized no more soggy left-over salads to be reluctantly tossed away. Darned clever, these bachelors.

When we finished our last ear of corn, Bob passed steaming hot washcloths, neatly folded in a wooden bowl for our sticky fingers. We nibbled on fresh fruit and cheese while lingering over hot black Java until we heard the soft notes of a piano and gradually, we drifted along with the rest of the guests back into the house, where some hummed old melodies around the piano and others stretched in front of the fireplace, which was banked just low enough to take the dampness out of the cool night air.

On the leisurely drive home that evening, I thought how lucky for us that Bob did not have a push-button automatic kitchen. For if he had, his originality and ingenuity would never have been challenged to create such a memorable evening for us in the land of Hiawatha. I have given below a luau menu inspired by Bob's party. Substitute mumus for Indian dress, and spareribs or pork for the roast pig, but *don't* forget the salad bar and the steaming washcloths.

Luau without Suckling Pig

Make-Your-Own Salad Bar (see above)

Fresh Corn on the Cob

Bar-B-Qued Spareribs or Sweet 'n' Sour Pork Chops

Corn Meal Sticks

Fresh Fruit and Berries with Assorted Cheeses and Crackers

Coffee

BAR-B-QUED SPARERIBS

Order three pounds baby-back spareribs and ask your butcher to cut the whole rib in 2" strips. Cut between ribs with scissors into individual pieces and place in a baking dish.

Sauce

2 tablespoons molasses
1 teaspoon Tabasco sauce
2 teaspoons vinegar or lemon juice
2 tablespoons prepared mustard
1 tablespoon soy sauce (or Kikkoman Hawaiian Teriyaki Sauce)

In a small bowl place molasses, add tabasco, blend well. Stir in vinegar, (or lemon juice), mustard and soy sauce. Brush over spareribs several times during baking. Bake in moderate oven 350° about 2 hours and transfer to chafing dish. Makes 12 servings

SWEET 'N' SOUR PORK CHOPS

Porky, the pig, landed in America long before the Mayflower, in fact, he was brought to the New World by Columbus and has flourished here ever since. This Pacific Island recipe is a summer treat in any part of the world.

    12 pork chops
    2 cans (13 1/2-oz. each) pineapple chunks
    2 cans (11-oz. each) mandarin oranges
    12 maraschino cherries
    1 cup vinegar
    1 cup light molasses
    1 teaspoon salt
    1/2 teaspoon ginger
    1 teaspoon soy sauce
    1 cup pineapple-orange syrup
    2 teaspoons water
    4 teaspoons cornstarch
    6 tablespoons diced green pepper

Place chops on rack in baking pan and bake in moderate oven, 325°F., for about an hour or until well done. Drain pineapple, oranges and cherries; reserve 1 cup syrup. Combine vinegar, molasses, salt, ginger, soy sauce and syrup in saucepan. Blend cornstarch with 2 teaspoons cold water until smooth, and add to molasses mixture. Add green pepper. Place over medium heat and bring to boil, then stir and reduce heat to simmer for 5 minutes. Add pineapple, oranges and cherries. Simmer for several minutes. Remove chops from oven and place on warm serving platter. Pour sauce over chops and serve. Makes 12 servings.

HOLIDAY AFTERMATHS

During the gay social holiday season, the smart homemaker, like a real boy scout, likes to "be prepared" for impromptu-entertaining. It's fun to be able to say when you're in a Mardi-Gras mood at a friend's cocktail party, "Why not come over to our house for a bite later?" knowing there's a kettle of Turkey Gumbo waiting to be warmed up at home. My New Orleans chums introduced the hearty gumbo to us and it's become a family stand-by ever since. It's the perfect way to turn turkey scraps and carcass into a dish fit for a king.

There's just one drawback to Gumbo: it needs filé powder (made from sassafras leaves), which isn't always available. (See Sources of Supply.)

The tamale pie is a dish which guests enjoy, winter and summer. Served with avocado salad and a light custard or flan, its fiesta quality is unmistakable.

Another uncomplicated holiday buffet centers around a cooked ham which is served with Lima Beans and Pear Casserole, and Camembert Salad á la Rothschild—both are refreshing changes from the usual dishes served with ham. The recipes follow.

TURKEY GUMBO

(New Orleans style without okra)

1 turkey carcass
2 stalks celery with greens
1 large onion
1 teaspoon salt
1/2 teaspoon pepper
1 level tablespoon shortening (Crisco, etc.)
1/3 cup chopped onion
2 tablespoons flour
1 or 2 teaspoons filé powder
1 cup raw long grain rice, cooked
    according to package directions

1. Remove nice chunks of dark and white meat from carcass to use later.

2. To make the broth take a large kettle and cover carcass with 3 quarts cold water. Add celery, onion, salt, pepper. Bring to boil then reduce heat and let simmer slowly for 2 hours. Strain.

3. Make roux by using a very large frying pan and heating shortening, mixing with chopped onion and flour. Add broth to

roux, stirring constantly until thick. Add small chunks of turkey meat.

4. Add filé powder but do not boil soup any longer, as turkey will become stringy.

5. Scoop rice into balls (with an ice cream scoop if you have one) and serve in soup bowl with hot gumbo. Makes about 10 servings.

TAMALE PIE

    1 lb. chopped beef
    1 tablespoon oil or shortening
    1/2 cup chopped onion
    1/2 cup chopped green pepper
    2 cans (15 oz. each) tomato sauce
    2 cloves garlic, minced or pressed
    1 tablespoon chili powder
    2 flakes red pepper, crushed
    1 can (1 lb. 12 oz.) kidney beans
    1 package "Jiffy" corn muffin
      mix (8 1/2 oz.)
    1 egg
    1/3 cup milk

Preheat oven to 400°F. Brown the meat in a medium-size skillet in shortening. Add onions, pepper, tomato sauce, garlic, chili powder, red pepper and cook over low heat for about 30 minutes. Stir occasionally. Add beans and remove from heat. Prepare cornmeal muffin batter according to directions on package with egg and milk. Pour meat and beans into 2 1/2-quart baking dish, cover top with corn-meal batter and bake for about 40 minutes or until top is brown. Serve piping hot. Makes 8 servings.

Addenda: The meat and bean mix may be prepared the day before and stored in the refrigerator or frozen.

LIMA BEANS AND PEAR CASSEROLE

    2 lbs. dried lima beans
    1/2 teaspoon salt
    2 cans (1 lb. 13 oz. each) Bartlett pear halves

1 cup melted butter
1 cup brown sugar
1/2 teaspoon powdered cinnamon
1/2 teaspoon clove or allspice
1 cup vinegar

Soak lima beans overnight in cold water. In a saucepan cover lima beans with salt water and cook about 20 minutes or until tender. Drain. Alternate lima beans with layers of pears in a 2-quart baking dish; add juice. Add melted butter, sugar, vinegar, cinnamon and clove and bake in 300°F. oven for 2 hours. Very tasty when reheated. Makes 12 servings.

CAMEMBERT SALAD A LA ROTHSCHILD

For buffet supper parties, the Camembert Salad à la Rothschild is a refreshing change from the usual tossed salad and may be served either as a salad or, the way Californians prefer, as a first course.

2 heads Boston lettuce
8 oz. Camembert cheese (room temperature)
2/3 cup chutney
1 cup French dressing
2 teaspoon paprika added
   to French dressing

Cut cheese and chutney with scissors into bite-size pieces. Add dressing and toss gently. Makes 12 servings.

NEW YEAR'S EVE:

The question, "What are you doing on New Year's?" almost always draws a spirited response. It seems to me that the people who argue the loudest about staying home alone seldom do; the people who try convincing anyone who'll listen that New Year's Eve is just like any other night—end up at the zero hour tooting their paper horns the loudest; the people who feel they can't bear to stay in town looking at the same old faces—run to resorts where they run into the same old faces; and even the people who make the least fuss over this emotion-charged holiday find that no matter how you look at it—New Year's Eve can be a problem. If you go out, it's terribly expensive. If you stay home, whom will you invite? If you're invited out, who's going to be there? If you go, do you have to stay? If you leave, where will you go?

One way to lick the dilemma is to plan a group party where each person or couple assumes part of the responsibility. It's

best to keep the group small, nine couples would be ideal for according to a University of Michigan research study, people function best in groups of sixes (nine couples compose three groups of sixes).

Assign each couple to bring a truly exotic dish (one could pick a nationality menu with a corresponding party theme). The cost of the liquor is then equally divided and the group either engages extra help to serve and clean up or uses attractive disposable paper goods.

Then too, it's best not to sit down to a big meal all at once because everyone gets sleepy and wants to go home. Instead stretch out each course through the evening, starting with cocktails and substantial hot hors d'oeuvres served up to about eleven o'clock; move on to a very light entrée or roast such as cold filets and a marinated vegetable salad platter, beautifully arranged in sections, and served in the living room, and wind up around two o'clock with coffee and sweets.

A successful variation of the above gourmet dinner is to make nine teams, splitting each couple in the process. Assign each team a job in preparing the meal. It's always surprising how many men enjoy demonstrating their skill with the skillet and it gives everyone something to do—but not too much! The host provides the supplies and has everything handy in the kitchen, including one or more cookbooks or typed directions for reference. It's a good idea to set up a time schedule on a blackboard which might look like this.

7:30	Team 1:	Mix and serve cocktails.
7:30	Team 2:	Prepare hors d'oeuvres.
8:00	Team 3:	Start charcoal fire and grill steaks when ready. (Or use broiler later.)
8:00	Team 4:	Bake potatoes; set the table.
8:15	Team 5:	Make ice cream in electric ice-cream freezer. Hostess prepares ice-cream base the day before.
8:30	Team 6:	Prepare salad and dressing.
8:45	Team 7:	Warm rolls and make coffee.
9:00	Team 8:	Host and hostess announce dinner is ready!
9:00	Team 9:	Serve dinner to guests.

FONDUE FUN

In February, especially on weekends, a persistent rat-tat-tat humming sound breaks the stillness of our moonlit nights on the quiet outskirts of Charlevoix. It's the sound of snowmobiles as they cut through wooded trails and snake their way over white hills and valleys, across open corn fields and along frosted Lake Michigan beaches. Not only in Northern Michigan, but all over the United States, snowmobile enthusiasts are skidoo-ing merrily in two's and four's over the rough terrain and man-made trails. Their numbers seem to multiply as fast as the rabbits who scurry nimbly out of their way.

My Swiss neighbors invited us to a Cheese Fondue supper (*fondue* is a French word that means to mix together) and the evening turned out to be a real mixer of not only cheese and wine but also of good food and fellowship.

Long before we sat down at a *gemütlich* round table in front of a fire, we were intrigued by the preparations that were under way in the kitchen where cheese was melting in a *caquelon,* as

the Swiss call their fondue dishes. These are made of earthenware with flat bottoms and hollow handles.

Our hostess explained that only the earthenware *caquelons* (no
copper or metal will do) can develop a heavenly crust which
forms on the bottom of the fondue dish and tastes like crisp
toasted cheese—so good and chewy! We could hardly contain
ourselves until the fortuitous moment when the *caquelon* was
transferred to the dining table and placed over an alcohol burner
and we were seated in a cozy circle just dipping away until there
wasn't another lick of cheese or a crust of bread. Not until the
flames in our grate fire had died very low did we reluctantly
leave the table and say our "adieus".

The Swiss consider fondue almost a meal in itself and they
usually serve only a little smoked ham or sausage afterward
followed by fresh fruit, such as apples or pears. (It's also a
marvelous dish to serve as a midnight snack after theater, movie,
or concert.)

Our hostess was more generous and here's our fondue dinner
menu.

Skidoo-Fondue Menu

Hors d'oeuvres: Romanoff pate (available in jars) and Crackers
Hickory Smoked Danish Ham (1-lb. can)

Spinach Salad with Anchovies
Cheese Fondue
Cubed French Bread

Kirsch   Tea or Coffee

Fresh Fruits (Pears, Apples, Black and White Grapes—grapes
may be frosted by dipping them wet in superfine XX granulated
sugar; chill in refrigerator.)

Crispy Lace Cookies (See Chapter III)

CHEESE FONDUE

People who know about this insist that imported Swiss Cheese must be used because American Swiss Cheese is not sufficiently matured to make a proper fondue. If one uses cheddar, be sure it is very mild, such as the Canadian cheddar.

1/2 lb. imported Swiss Cheese (Emmentaler)
1/2 lb. Gruyere or mild cheddar
4 teaspoons flour
1 clove garlic
2 cups dry white wine (Neuchatel, Riesling or Chablis)
1/4 cup Kirschwasser (no substitute)
2 teaspoons cornstarch
Dash of nutmeg, salt and pepper
         (Methyl alcohol for burner)

1. Trim edges of cheese. Cut cheese in 1/2-inch cubes and dredge lightly with flour by putting them in a paper bag with flour, and shaking. Rub *caquelon* with garlic. Pour wine in *caquelon* and heat very slowly until air bubbles rise but do *not* boil. Add a handful of cheese cubes and stir with a wooden spoon in a figure 8 waiting until each handful is melted before adding more cheese. Keep stirring (about 15 minutes) until all cheese is smooth and fondue is thickened and bubbling slightly. Now add Kirschwasser (if the fondue is thinner than you'd like it, stir 2 teaspoons cornstarch into the Kirschwasser—not into the fondue or it will be lumpy!) Fondue may be cooked on the stove and then transferred to the alcohol burner on the table if one wishes. Add nutmeg, salt and pepper.

2. Cut very crusty French bread into bite-size pieces, wrap in foil and heat in oven until warm.

3. Each person uses a long fondue fork for dipping bread into cheese.

4. Be sure to warn everyone not to touch the bottom of the caquelon when dipping because one of the rituals of the fondue bit is to allow a crust to form on the bottom of the dish. This begins as soon as one stops stirring and when there is sufficient heat causing the cheese to bubble. When you feel the crust forming, you can very carefully lift the nice brown crust off the bottom with a fork without breaking it and serve it to your guests.

But if the crust is disturbed during the dipping it will come up into the fondue in little crusty pieces and spoil the looks of the fondue and the crust itself. The consistency of Cheese Fondue is similar to chocolate syrup and it's much milder and more delicate in taste than Welsh Rarebit. Serves 4 persons for dinner; 12 for cocktails.

Addenda: This is one recipe that's better not doubled because it takes the cheese too long to melt. Instead use 2 *caquelons*.

As an hors d'oeuvre

Cheese fondue served as a cocktail or midnight snack is delicious with crabmeat mixed into the fondue, then spread on toasted rounds or served with torn toasted bits of sourdough bread speared with a fondue fork.

With fresh fruit

Fresh, chilled winter pears, either the Anjou, Bosc or Comice, are wonderfully compatible with cheese fondue either as a dipper or dessert. A pear cutter (available at any hardware store) is handy for slicing the juicy fresh pears into thick even wedges. Or provide your guests with dessert knives.

A perfect dessert for this continental supper is a colorful platter of pears, apples, grapes or dried raisins and nuts.

SPINACH SALAD

1 package fresh spinach
1/2 lb. crisp bacon bits
1 small Bermuda onion, sliced thin
6 radishes, sliced thin
1/2 cup vinegar
1/2 cup water
1/2 cup sugar
1/2 teaspoon salt
1 egg, well beaten
3 hard-cooked eggs, sliced
2 cans anchovies

Wash and dry spinach thoroughly with a towel. Remember the dressing won't cling to water! Add bacon bits, onion and radishes. Make dressing: Pour vinegar, water, sugar and salt into small pan. In a small mixing bowl, beat one whole egg with egg beater or wire whisk. Add to small pan and bring to boil. Let cool and pour over tossed salad ingredients. Garnish with sliced hard-cooked eggs and anchovies. Makes 8 servings.

Dinners with a Flair

"All human history attests
That happiness for man—the hungry sinner
Since Eve ate apples,
Much depends on dinner."—Lord Byron

STRETCHING ONE'S HOUSE

"Oh, I wish we could give a lovely dinner party—but where to put everyone? There isn't enough room! It's impossible! I just can't begin to manage!" Does this sound like you?

If so, your problem is not unique. During the Kennedy term in the White House, Jacqueline Kennedy ingeniously doubled the seating arrangement for State Dinners making it possible to invite twice the number of guests! No fairy godmother stretched the White House formal dining room nor will one wave her magic wand and turn your efficient apartment into a king-size chateau, or your compact ranch-style, bi-level into a spacious palace, or your cozy Cape Cod cottage into a rambling castle, but there are calculated ways of s-t-r-e-t-c-h-i-n-g your home so that you can comfortably double or even triple the number of guests.

Better yet, you can do it without turning yourself into a drudge. The hostess always plays the lead in every party production, so enjoy yourself cast in the glamorous role of star.

How do we stretch a house or a mansion? Let's mentally clear all furniture from the room. (Of course, there are some people who actually do put their furniture in storage for a couple of days when giving a gala ball at home, but that doesn't concern us now.) Let's pretend we're designing a· set from scratch. Walk around your imaginary bare stage and do a little creative play acting. Let's see—guests enter here—or do they? Sometimes traffic patterns can be changed to advantage by using an alternate entrance or by setting up portable coat racks for hats and coats. The bar should be located against the long wall because this is where most people like to congregate (and sometimes it's a good idea to set up an auxiliary bar). Shall we move the couch over a little and turn the table the other way? Let's dispose of that dainty chair and tippy table and avoid accidents.

What about the dining area? Is there enough room for waitresses to pass platters or shall we plan a serve-self buffet? Maybe we should not set any places at all but serve finger food or lap food—no knives required. Whatever decision we reach, avoid bringing in a filled dinner plate from the kitchen. It's so institutional! Letting people help themselves is so much more gracious.

For sit-down dinners we have the choice of extending our dining table by adding a card table or folding aluminum table on one end. A friend of mine from Washington stretched her dining-room table to accommodate fourteen instead of twelve by simply exchanging her commodious dining-room chairs for a set of fourteen rented smaller gilt chairs.

Or we can completely clear the dining area for cocktails and set up either a long table or several card tables in the living room. Card tables are especially handy for those challenging after-dinner bridge games. Or we can rent folding circular table tops that fit over card tables, they come in two sizes to accommodate either six or eight persons.

Her Serene Highness, Princess Grace of Monaco has introduced the *diner par petites tables* for those occasions when protocol does not need to be observed at the Palace. (We'll tell you more about her formal-style entertaining in Chapter VII.) On these less than formal occasions, Princess Grace enjoys using embroidered white organdy cloths with rose or yellow linen "petticoats" falling clear to the ground, with centerpieces of three-branched silver candlesticks surrounded by pastel-colored flowers arranged usually with small tea roses, sweetpeas or carnations.

Another way to double the space in a dining room as I once did for a series of buffet dinner parties is to order an eight-foot plywood board which we set up on two wooden horses across a small credenza along a long wall. Over this we spread a large white damask cloth that hung almost to the floor, completely covering both the credenza and wooden horses. This spacious sideboard gave us plenty of room for plates, hot trays, covered vegetable dishes and platters. We could easily seat twelve at the dining-room table and ten at a folding table in the adjoining breakfast room. On informal occasions for young people, everyone helped themselves to second servings from our improvised sideboard, but for more formal dinners, waitresses passed second helpings on platters and cleared the table for dessert and coffee. Remember to allow sufficient room between chairs for large platters to be passed or diners will be bending uncomfortably from side to side like sheaves of wheat in a storm. Better to invite one or two couples less and not overcrowd those present.

Poet William Allingham rhymes it: "Solitude is very sad, but too much company is twice as bad!"

On another occasion we stretched our house for a "June-in-January" party by decorating a basement room with hand-painted murals. Here we served cocktails to our delighted guests who wandered about the room pointing themselves out to each other as sketched in resort scenes comic-strip fashion. There's the traditional golfer complaining "I was on in two and took three putts!" and the tennis player who always loses wailing. "The score was point set and my partner served doubles twice!" and becalmed sailors unsuccessfully hailing sunbathers on a beach deeply engrossed in reading books with the most unlikely titles! I can't begin to tell you who had more fun, those of us who planned the mural or our flattered guests because we fussed!

Party consultants have a dozen clever tricks up their sleeves and know how to stretch a house by taking advantage of an enclosed porch or hallway where one can store an extra table that is completely set for dinner only to be whisked out just when everyone is ready to sit down. Only the water glasses need filling. I once attended a huge garden party where the garage was turned into a serving pantry—a handy plan that later saved hundreds of steps.

But that's nothing compared to the ingenuity of two mini-apartment dwellers who solve the kitchen space race by developing a mutual assistance pact that would shame most U.N. delegates. Both apartments are located just across the hall from one another and whenever one couple entertains, the other takes charge of the clean up. This reciprocal system is so refined through practice that all the used dishes are stacked on a card table in the tiny kitchen and in minutes Mr. and Mrs. Neighbor step in, whisk the table away, dishes and all, to be returned clean and dry.

With creative planning and the aid of modern accessories, entertaining can be a breeze. One could weep when one sees people doing things the hard way.

WHO NEEDS PLACE CARDS?

Place cards are a convenience when there are more than six guests, because who likes to stand around while the hostess muses, *ad nauseum,* "John please sit here, no, I think you'd better sit over there—no, I was right in the first place, do sit over here!"

Place cards are a boon to a thoughtful hostess because instead of allowing people who see a lot of each other to gyrate in the same direction and end up in the same little groups, she gives her guests the pleasure of meeting new people whom they will enjoy.

There's another advantage a friend of mine cleverly employs at her most successful parties. When she sees a couple engrossed in conversation during the cocktail hour she manages to draw the lady aside and whisper, "John's your dinner partner so save your chit-chat for later, darling!" A thousand blessings on her perceptive head!

Place cards can be fun at informal luncheons or dinners. My mother once invited a group of friends for lunch after recuperating from an operation and with her usual originality used her "Get-Well" cards as place cards. This idea prompted me that winter to save post cards from traveling friends, to use as place cards for a welcome home party. What memories these little cards evoked! "Remember that cute little place—what was it called?" "That's where we had dinner with that charming couple from Australia!" and so forth.

One can collect baby pictures of each guest in advance, or one can cut pictures from magazines highlighting each person's hobby, profession or idiosyncrasy. One can take Polaroid pictures of arriving guests and use them as place cards; one can write a couplet or a ditty, or sketch matchstick figures or paint holiday designs on each place card; one can glue a tiny flower or piece of cloth that carries out the party theme on a plain white folded card; one can use place card holders made of plastic, ceramic, wood or shells.

When planning your seating arrangements, remember that the gentleman guest of honor is always seated at the hostess's right and a lady guest of honor is seated to the host's right. After this, scatter gay talkers and sober listeners with studied indifference, but never invite people knowingly who are not on good terms. They'll have a miserable time ducking each other!

When seating an even number of men and women at the table, notice that whenever there are four or any number divided by four—such as eight, twelve, sixteen etc.—it works out mathematically that a man sits at the head and foot of the table. When there are six, ten, fourteen, it works out that a man sits at the head and a woman at the foot of the table.

There's no hard and fast rule that the host and hostess must be at the head and foot of the table. At the Belgian Embassy in Washington, D.C. a former Ambassador and his wife, Baron and Baroness Silvercruys, often sat opposite each other at the center of the table.

Finally, do place yourself facing the serving pantry door so you may signal the waiter without turning around.

SERVING ENGLISH STYLE

This could be called how to handle the whole show alone or with your husband's help!

At a recent dinner, poor Jane scurried between the kitchen and dining room during the entire meal. Bowls and platters circled the table as if they were riding a merry-go-round. Conversation was impossible except for "thank you" or "may I pass you this?" Heads turned left and right as if everyone were viewing a Davis Cup Match. What a harrowing experience! The service would have been so much smoother if Jane had served English style. After appetizers or first course are finished in the living room (and the cocktail clutter unobtrusively cleared) everyone moves to the dining room where the salad, butter and butter plates are waiting on the table; water glasses filled; candles lit. Meat, vegetables, potatoes and warm dinner plates are handy at an adjacent serving table. We love our attractive electric plate-cozy that keeps as many as a dozen plates warm. If you like the look of a service plate at every place as guests sit down (and I do!) then set the table that way but, for all practical purposes, without help the extra plate only adds to confusion. The host fills each plate for the guest inquiring, "Do you prefer your meat rare or well done?" or "dark or light meat?" or some such question, then offers the plate to his guest. Only rolls need passing.

At dessert time a tea wagon or triple-tiered cart is invaluable for quick service. On the cart, ready and waiting, Jane has pre-

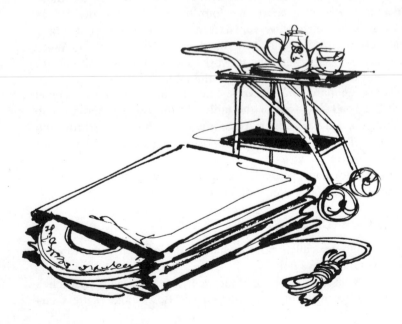

viously placed cups, saucers, dessert plates, cake server, knife, creamer and sugar. She first clears the main course from the serving table (first trip to the kitchen) and shifts the dessert cups, etc. from the cart to the serving table. This now leaves the cart clear for the used dinner plates which she removes from the dining table, stacks on the cart and wheels into the kitchen. (This system also leaves her valuable kitchen counter space during clean-up time). She returns to the dining room with dessert, nothing that needs to be scooped out or unmolded, and lets one of her guests do the honors of cutting the cake or pie, while Jane is free to sit down and pour coffee at her usual place.

Sometimes Jane might prefer to invite everyone to adjourn to the living room for a demi-tasse of coffee, dessert and brandy. Or a sweet combination of coffee, brandy and whipped cream— Irish Coffee.

Serving English style accomplishes three purposes. Entertaining becomes a pleasure because it keeps Jane with her guests most of the time and gives her an opportunity to listen and perhaps steer the conversation to light generalities, and it also gives her guests the comfortable feeling of being entertained graciously by the lady of the house and not by a drudge.

WHAT TO DO ABOUT LATECOMERS?

Speaking of delay, I'd like to share with you a comment on the manners and *mores* of the day in English society. It comes from a delightful little book, *Apician Morsels,* printed in 1834:

"If, by any unforeseen accident, any fortuitous circumstance, the moment of dining be put off for only one hour, just look at your guests, and twig what long faces they make; see how the most animated conversation languishes, how blue everyone looks, how all zygomatic muscles are paralysed, in short, how every eye appears mechanically turned toward the dining-room! Is the obstacle removed? the master of the hotel, a napkin under his arm, comes to announce that all is ready and served up; the words act like a charm—they have a magical effect which restores to each his serenity, his gaiety, and wit. An appetite is read in every eye, hilarity in every heart; and the tumultous impatience with which each runs to take possession of his plate, is a manifest and certain sign

*of the unanimity of wishes and the correspondence of sen-
sations. Nature then resumes all her rights: and at that moment
of the day, the flatterer himself suffer his thought to be read
in every feature of his countenance. The longing looks, the
smacking of lips, the anxious expectation, which are every
where visible, paint the conflict of the belly-gerent powers,
eager for the attack."*

The other side of the coin (when the host is kept waiting too
long) has been a problem even in Dr. Samuel Johnson's day. It
was Boswell who said,

*"One of the company not being come at the appointed hour, I
proposed, as usual upon such occasions, to order dinner to be
served, adding, 'Ought six people be kept waiting for one?'
    'Why, yes , answered Johnson, with a delicate humanity
'if the one will suffer more by your not sitting down, then the
six will do by waiting.' "*

Today's hep hostesses overcome cocktail bottleneck delays by
mailing invitations that read, "Cocktails at 7:00—Dinner at 8:00".
There's no excuse now for carefree guests wandering in thirty
or forty minutes late, causing a frenzied hostess to juggle pots
and pans in the kitchen, or for famished guests to stand around
while latecomers catch up with their drinks and hors d'oeuvres.

And speaking of hors d'oeuvres, with a substantial sit-down
dinner, there's no need to ruin everyone's appetite with a large
hearty variety. Just a few nibbles of fresh or imported cheese, or
a shrimp dip or pickled rainbow trout fit the bill nicely.

TIME AND TIDE WAIT FOR NO MAN—
BUT ROAST BEEF DOES!

One of the easiest main dishes to prepare . . . and a sure
guest-pleaser . . . is a standing rib roast.

Without a doubt the most important pointer when planning a
roast is to be sure it is timed properly, for a too-well-done roast
beef has thrown even the most experienced hostess for the pro-
verbial loop. How to avoid this trap is so divinely simple, it's
positively foolproof.

If you love your meat rare in the middle as we do, figure
exactly 15 minutes per pound and *never cook over 2 1/2 hours—*

no matter how heavy the roast! After removing the roast from the oven *always* allow at least 20 minutes for the roast to set before carving. As any fine chef will tell you, this method keeps the juices *in* the meat and *off* the platter. Besides it's far better to remove the roast from the oven when it's tender and serve it rare at room temperature, than to keep it warm and serve it dried out and over-cooked. When your plates are nice and warm and your gravy is piping hot and your meat is pink and juicy— your meal can't help but be a triumph. (The same rules apply when preparing strip filet.)

Let's say you have a 6 lb. rib roast at room temperature to put in a preheated oven for 1 1/2 hrs. (Rare takes 15 minutes a pound). Allowing an additional 20 minutes for the roast to set before carving means if you're planning to eat at 7:30, the roast should go in the oven at 5:40 o'clock. The 20 minutes setting time gives you the needed time to prepare the gravy. Don't be afraid to keep your roast beef waiting, covered with a sheet of aluminum foil until you're good and ready to serve, but remember there's no need to hold up dinner for anyone except the guest of honor and even then not for more than twenty minutes.

The Never-Fail Dinner Menu

Pickled Rainbow or Brook Trout (see Chapter IV)
Standing Rib Roast and Gravy
Roast Potatoes with Onions
or
Individual Yorkshire Pudding
Baked Apricot Joy
Green Spinach Salad (See Chapter V)
Mousse au Chocolat with Ladyfingers or Irish Coffee

RARE ROAST BEEF

For rare roast beef allow 15 minutes to the pound roasting time. (For medium done beef allow 20 minutes to the pound). Plus *at least* an extra 20 minutes for the meat to set!

Season meat (which should be at room temperature) with salt and a lot of paprika. Place in roasting pan *fat side up* in 500°F. oven for 20 minutes without water. Reduce heat to 300° and baste occasionally with fat drippings.

Remove from oven and place roast on platter and allow to set. Cover with aluminum foil until ready to carve into slices one-half or three-quarters of an inch thick.

Place the unwashed roasting pan on range. We will use this pan for making a ten-minute gravy.

ROAST BEEF GRAVY

Remove all but about 2 tablespoons of drippings from roasting pan and place on range over low heat. Add one teaspoon flour, teaspoon each of Worcestershire sauce and A-1 sauce, 1/4 cup chili sauce, salt and pepper. Add a cup of water and with a wooden spoon stir slowly for several minutes until all the brown juice that sticks to the pan is dissolved. This brown juice from the pan is the secret of making a superior gravy. Cook over a very low flame for ten minutes, or until you are ready to serve. If the gravy gets too thick add more water, if too thin add a little more flour. (Quantities will vary—the method won't!) By the way, the roast beef bones make a fine soup stock, see index for recipe.

GOLDEN ROAST POTATOES

Too often when one thinks of roast potatoes, one thinks of potatoes that have been cooked in gravy, such as a pot roast, which causes them to turn brown and soft. However, when one roasts potatoes with a roast beef where they don't come in contact with any liquid, and if one bastes them occasionally with the fat drippings—ah! these potatoes are something quite different because they turn crisp and gold.

Peel medium-size potato and place around roast from the start. With a small roast it may be necessary to cut the potatoes in half for faster cooking. Baste occasionally with fat drippings. (The ball tube prevents one from burning oneself). In about one hour begin testing with fork to see if done. When done, remove from oven and keep warm in covered pan on top of stove or in warming oven.

BAKED ONIONS

Peel medium-size onions and add to roasting pan only for the last hour. (Figure one or two per person).

After one has sufficiently mastered the roast beef routine, it's possible to substitute Yorkshire Pudding for the potatoes if one wants to, all this with one oven, too! You can make it from a mix or start from scratch as you wish. Plan to make your batter an hour or more ahead so that after you've removed the roast from the oven to let it set, before you start with the gravy (and while your guests are on their second cocktail) you can whip individual Yorkshire Pudding into the oven just like that! (Individual Yorkshire Pudding resembles popovers.)

YORKSHIRE PUDDING

1 cup all-purpose flour
1/2 teaspoon salt
1 tablespoon butter or vegetable shortening
1 cup milk
2 eggs
1/4 cup roast beef drippings or melted shortening

Sift flour (even pre-sifted flour) and salt into bowl of electric mixer. Cut in 1 tablespoon shortening and cream well. Add milk and eggs and beat on high speed for 10 minutes. Chill thoroughly in refrigerator for at least one hour. Half an hour before serving turn oven to 425° and place empty popover or muffin tins in oven until very hot. Pour about a teaspoon of roast drippings in each and fill half full with batter. Bake in 425° oven for 30 minutes and serve at once. Makes 12 servings.

BAKED APRICOT JOY

This dish somewhat resembles in consistency the tomato pudding described in Chapter V. We like to serve it in small vegetable saucers as a side dish instead of a vegetable because it may be prepared the day before or kept on hand frozen.

    1 lb. tenderized apricots
    4 cups water
    1/2 cup butter
    4 slices dry bread, no crust
    1 cup brown sugar, packed

    1. Place apricots in uncovered saucepan. Add cold water and bring to a boil. Simmer gently for 30 minutes uncovered. Let cool and reserve liquid.

    2. Preheat oven to 300°F. Butter a 2-quart casserole generously. Place a layer of stewed apricots on bottom. Add layer of bread cut into 1 1/2 inch squares and sprinkle with brown sugar. Continue making layers until ingredients are all used up. Moisten with liquid from stewing. Bake covered in oven for 35 minutes. (When re-heating it may be necessary to add 1/4 cup of water and stir). Makes 10 servings.

MOUSSE AU CHOCOLAT

    My do-it-yourself dinner parties always include a dessert that doesn't need assembling at the last minute. For instance I'd never fool with ice-cream and hot fudge sauce and cookies. Just think of all the time and steps involved!—removing the ice cream from refrigerator—scooping it into individual sauce dishes—heating the chocolate and pouring the sauce over the ice cream—placing the sauce dishes on a plate then on a tray and adding the cookies;—and carrying the tray into the dining room. Much better to reduce these five steps to two by opening the refrigerator and carrying a cake, pudding or pie to the dining room.

    This may be prepared in the morning or the day before. It's almost too rich for encores.

    1/4 lb. bitter chocolate
    1/4 lb. semi-sweet chocolate
    3/4 cup powdered sugar
    1/4 cup water
    5 eggs
    1 teaspoon vanilla
    Whipped cream (optional)

    Melt together in double boiler chocolates, sugar and water. Stir until smooth and velvety and thoroughly blended. Remove

top of double boiler from heat and set in a pan of cold water
Stir occasionally until mixture is cool. Separate eggs. Beat yolks
well in a small bowl. Add vanilla and blend with chocolate mixture which should be semi-fluid. (If too firm, add 4 or 5 tablespoons tepid milk). Beat egg whites until stiff and fold into chocolate mixture, gently, but thoroughly. Chill for 6-8 hours. Fills a
9" x 12" oval serving dish, or may be poured into individual
sherbet glasses. Decorate with whipped cream if you like. Makes
12 servings.

IRISH COFFEE

Fill a parfait glass or an old-fashioned glass with strong coffee,
stir well with a lump of sugar. Add a jigger of scotch, bourbon
or Irish whiskey. Top with a dash of whipped cream and serve
hot.

PROGRESSIVE PARTIES

There's nothing political in planning a progressive party—it's
just a convenient way for two or three or more couples to entertain elegantly, especially when they live within easy walking or
a short driving distance from each other. Try to pick a fair weather month; walking from house to house when flowers are in
bloom or the leaves are turning is a lark, but in foul weather,
pulling galoshes or snow boots off and on all evening is a drag!

A progressive party, like a well-structured play, is divided
into two, three or more acts. The first act opens with cocktails
and hors d'oeuvres followed by intermission, when guests proceed to the next house for the second act where entrée or roast
and dessert are served, or a third act could wind up with dessert
and dancing in another location.

The advantages here are obvious, each hostess is responsible
for only one course instead of providing an entire meal plus
entertainment. However, there are pitfalls. With a progressive
party there must be perfect co-operation and teamwork between
hostesses to keep the entire group moving smoothly on schedule
from one home on to the next. When it's time to leave it might
be wise to dim the lights momentarily as is done in theater
lobbies, or to ring a bell announcing that it's time for the next
act to begin.

Progressive parties can be tied into fund-raising house tours; plan them around ethnic themes so that each house has related party decorations and food. Or the theme can go back to American history—as seventeenth century party with a pioneer style; eighteenth century with Colonial elegance; nineteenth century Victorianism; and space-age modernity.

SPLIT EXPENSES AND DOUBLE THE FUN!

I find party-giving a lot less worrisome when we share the fun of planning and doing, along with the advantage of splitting expenses with another couple. Many people find that co-hosting a party is also advantageous for newcomers in a community who may not be familiar with all the local "ins and outs", as well as for native sons whose space, budget and guest list are not in balance.

Planning

Once the selection of a congenial co-host or hosts has been made, there are two choices. 1) The proposed party can begin and end at the same address or 2) the progressive party can move from one house to another—but more about that later.

In either case, preparations, party chores and party clean-up, as well as expenses, should be shared equally.

Preparation

If the party is to be given at our house, we have a greater responsibility in getting ready, and consequently our co-hosts should assume extra chores, such as ordering flowers, writing place cards, arranging games after dinner and/or addressing invitations.

Just Another Word About Invitations!

When a party is co-hosted, it's better to send written invitations. Too many beautiful friendships have been strained when guests have been invited over the phone or a little too casually without it being made crystal clear that the party is being co-hosted. Only one return address is necessary, because it's simpler for one person to keep track of all acceptances and regrets.

Party Themes

Creating a mood, an atmosphere, is a key to giving a party with character and individuality. Will it be a bright bash, a swing and sway, or a harvest-moon mood? Now is the time to co-ordinate a timely or amusing party theme by choosing appropriate invitations, decorations, music, entertainment and menu. (See Chapter IX on party themes.)

Budget

In order to prevent any future unpleasantness, it's best to decide now if the party will be geared to beer-on-tap or champagne standards. Whatever you decide, always serve the best quality, whether it is apple cider, ale or whiskey.

When dividing financial responsibilities, some people like to keep a duplicate list and an accurate record of every penny spent, i.e., 1 lb. butter, 1 pt. cream, 1 tablecloth laundered, etc., while others are quite content to be extremely casual and say, "We'll supply the liquor and food, and you take care of the orchestra and flowers," or some such thing. A third group falls somewhere between these two. Leafing through my party diary, my notes look something like this:

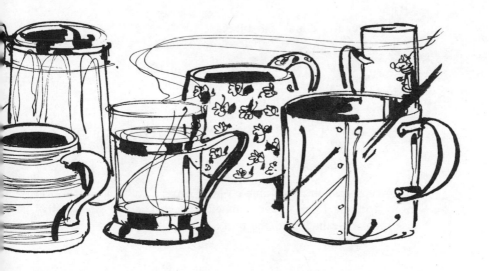

Date _____   Co-hosts _____   How Many?

Place _____   Occasion _____

LIQUOR	2 cases	$XXX.xx
FOOD Bakery	Birthday Cake 100 rolls 4 rye breads	X.xx
Butcher	2 hams, 2 turkeys 2 lbs. chicken livers	XX.xx
Grocery	3 dips, cheeses, coffee, etc.	XX.xx
CATERESS Mrs. Cateress 2 waitresses	2 casseroles 4 ring molds	XX.xx
BARTENDERS Mike & Bill	Ice	XX.xx
RENTAL **EQUIPMENT**	Bar, chairs, dishes, glasses, silverware	XX.xx
MUSIC University Band	3 pieces 9 P.M. to 1 A.M.	XXX.xx
Misc.	Candles, cig., matches, candy, laundry, flowers, etc.	XX.xx

TOTAL $XXX.xx

Our Share   XXX.xx

A memorandum from our co-hosts says, "Although there was more drinking than we anticipated, the cost is still about 50% less than if we had held the party at the club."

ACT I

Showmanship means "hooking" an audience with a solid opening scene, and good showmanship is as fruitful in the social world as it is in the theatrical one. The beat of music, live or recorded, is an added boon that helps get a swinging party off the ground quickly. The artistic host, responsible only for the cocktail hour, has a superb opportunity to "hook" his guests with a marvelous display of hors d'oeuvres (See Chapter IV) and a glamorous drink to suit the occasion. Of course, it's impossible to list here all the exotic fun drinks. Almost any fair-sized book on mixed drinks contains hundreds of recipes. We have mentioned only a few popular mixed drinks in Chapter IV and several basic punches in Chapter III. But there are many unusual chilled summer drinks to choose from: shrubs, coolers, collins, fizzes or punches; or hot winter toddies, grogs or nogs.

Throw caution to the winds and enchant your guests with a specialty of the house by using an unusual container or garnish. You might decide to frost the rim of a glass with sugar for Daiquiris or salt for Margaritas. Or you may prefer to vary the

regulation glass with an attractive plastic or paper print, but then it's best to add a straw; most people don't care to sip a drink from a paper or plastic cup. For variety insert a glass in a half a grapefruit, pineapple or coconut shell filled with crushed ice. Or use cups, mugs, or tankards made of china, pewter or glass.

Finally, the piece de résistance is a decorative perky garnish on your "specialty" made of a sprig of fresh mint, a few leaves of borage, sweet woodruff, lemon balm, or scented geranium. One may use fresh strawberries or slices of pineapple, lemon, lime or orange. One may use maraschino cherries, olives, pickled onions —or fresh flower blossoms as they do in Hawaii.

ACT II

Every stage producer knows that a sound first act does not guarantee the success of a play. Holding the audience in their seats depends greatly on the second act and for a successful progressive dinner it's best to plan a menu that will "hold" in the oven, too. An overdone roast beef or a limp soufflé is an avoidable tragedy!

Instead, an excellent choice for a cocktail supper might be Indian Curried Shrimp or Rijsttafel with assorted condiments, because 1) it's something different and 2) there's no need to fear that the food will melt or wilt or dry out. Everything is cooked and arranged ahead of time leaving a carefree hostess to enjoy the cocktail hour.

Reluctant to serve a curried dish? Afraid too many people won't enjoy it? Better stick to the old tried and true? Oh, no! It's perfectly astonishing how popular curried foods are even among the uninitiated. I've seen them return again and again for second and third helpings. (But you can have on hand some fried or roast chicken or stewed breast of chicken or some such thing for the rare guest whose diet is strictly limited.)

This menu has another advantage. Exotic Indian dishes are so easy to display with a flair. Use an inexpensive Indian paisley tablecloth, add brass candle holders, and at one end of the table, borrow if you must, two brass or china bowls. Fill one with curried shrimp and the other with rice sprinkled with parsley. Invest in a dozen inexpensive oriental bowls. (They can be used again for outdoor barbecues, filled with mustard, catsup, pickles, relishes and other condiments.) Each bowl holds nuts, coconut, etc. Place the small bowls in a semi-circle around a basket of golden crescent rolls and introduce your guests to a new taste thrill. Suggest they try a sampling of whatever condiment appeals, but chutney, of course, is essential.

There are many curried dishes to choose from in addition to shrimp. There's lamb or veal, chicken, turkey, duck, capon.

Act II, Menu For 32

Shrimp Curry

Fried Chicken   Rice with Parsley

Assorted Accompaniments

Wine: Graves Royal   Crescent Rolls

Tea   Coffee

Accompaniments Eight-ounce bowls of: Seedless Raisins; Sweet Pickles, diced; Slivered Almonds; Grated Coconut; Grated Orange Rind; Chopped Black Olives; Grated Egg Yolk; Chopped Bacon; Chopped Egg White; Chopped Peanuts. Larger bowls of: Pineapple Chunks and Chutney (4 bottles); plan on refilling these bowls.

SHRIMP CURRY

    12 lbs. shrimp
    1 cup finely chopped onion
    3 cups butter
    3 cups flour
    8 tablespoons curry powder
    12 cups (3 quarts) coconut milk, canned (see following
        recipe) or dilute 2 cups powdered coconut in 3 quarts
        milk
    4 teaspoons ground ginger
    2/3 cup lemon juice
    4 tablespoons salt

1. Shell and de-vein shrimp.

2. Sauté onion in butter in large saucepan for 5 minutes. Stir in flour and curry powder. Add coconut milk and cook over low heat until thickened, stirring constantly. (Coconut milk is very sensitive to high heat.)

3. Add shrimp, ginger, lemon juice, and salt. Simmer uncovered for 30 minutes, stirring frequently. Place in refrigerator.

4. Reheat just before serving. Add plain milk if required.

Addenda: This may be prepared a day ahead. Also a good curry recipe to use with cooked lean fish or hard-cooked eggs.

Although many of us know what curry powder looks, smells and tastes like, few know what it actually is—a blend of from five to fifty spices capable of almost infinite variation, including black and white pepper, cayenne, chili, cinnamon, nutmeg, cloves, allspice, poppy seeds, fenugreek, cardamom, coriander, fennel, cumin, turmeric, ginger and saffron. Compare three or four of the better-known brands before settling on just any old curry powder.

COCONUT MILK

Coconut milk in liquid and powdered form is available at most food specialty stores, or substitute 12 cups shredded canned coconut soaked in 12 cups milk. Let stand at room temperature for 20 minutes, bring to a boil, then reduce heat immediately and let simmer for 10 more minutes. Strain milk through a cheesecloth and discard shredded coconut. Or select 6 fresh coconuts that are heavy with liquid. To remove meat, first drain the liquid by opening 2 eyes at one end with an ice pick. Tap the coconut with a hammer to loosen meat from the shell, before breaking open. The meat should fall out in large chunks. Pry off any pieces that cling to the shell with a knife. Peel off brown skin with a sharp knife and grate coconut by hand or in a blender. (For blender, cut into small slices about 1/4 inch thick.) In a saucepan bring to boil, 3 cups milk and 6 cups cream. Place 1 cup diced coconut in blender with 1/2 cup hot cream-milk mixture. Cover and turn on high speed for 8 seconds. Pour into bowl and repeat process until all coconut meat and cream mixture is used. Cool. Pour through cheesecloth and discard coconut. Makes 12 cups.

ACT III

All heads turn when a flaming dessert is the grand finale on the program. It's a dramatic and delicious climax for a progressive cocktail supper and is sure to win the enthusiastic applause of every party-goer. Here's a golden opportunity to use, rent or borrow a lovely chafing dish (an electric frypan or a copper skillet over a hot plate will do nicely) and taking a leaf from the great French restauranteurs, to perform a bit of legerdemain for guests.

Arrange everything needed in advance on a separate table or hostess cart and never yield to the temptation *ever* to ignite a flaming dessert in the kitchen or to carry it in like a birthday cake, because the flame rarely lasts until you reach the dining room. Besides, mixing the sauce and pouring the brandy and lighting the flame is all so much a part of the total performance —it must be done on-stage and not in the wings!

There are two simple keys to success when serving any flaming dessert or coffee.

1. Dim the lights low to achieve the greatest visual effect. (Unplug the electric skillet too, for safety.)

2. Have everything *hot*, including the spoon with which you ignite the brandy.

Preparing Crêpes Suzette may sound scary to some, but once you've prepared this gourmet dish you'll want to serve it often for if you can swing a golf club, you can swing an omelet pan! Remember, a crepe is nothing more than a pancake composed of a batter made with eggs, flour, and milk and poured sparingly into a frying pan and fried on both sides. Simple?

Crepes can be made weeks before and frozen between sheets of wax paper and wrapped in freezer wrap. All one need do on the morning of the party is to make the sauce and add it to the crepes, which are then rolled or folded into quarters. Before serving, place them in the oven at 350° to warm.

There are many variations of crepe batter and fillings besides the one recommended here. Alsatian crepes are filled with raspberry jelly, sprinkled with sugar and glazed with raspberry jelly and placed in a hot oven. For breakfast, any fresh fruit may be served with crepes without the liquor; strawberries, bananas, apricots, blueberries, etc.

As a luncheon dish, eliminate the sugar in the batter and fill crepes with a variety of cheeses such as Roquefort, cream cheese or sour cream.

But let's get back to Crepes Suzette which is so elegant served as dessert or at midnight on New Year's Eve.

CREPES SUZETTE

> 2 level cups sifted flour
> 2 tablespoons sugar
> 6 eggs, beaten
> 1 cup clarified butter or polyunsaturated vegetable oil
> (most of this is used to brown the crepes in the pan)
> 1 quart milk
> 3 or 4 drops vanilla flavoring

1. Make batter: In a large bowl, combine flour and sugar. Beat eggs in a separate, medium-size bowl and add 6 tablespoons of clarified butter (to clarify butter: melt in a small container, skim off foam, pour off and reserve fat and discard sediment in bottom of container) or oil; add milk and vanilla. Pour liquid into flour, gradually mixing until batter is smooth, using wire whisk or egg beater. Let batter stand for at least one hour. Add milk as batter thickens.

2. Heat a 5- or 6-inch omelet pan or iron skillet and melt 1 teaspoon of clarified butter. Measure a tablespoon or so of batter into pan with a small circular motion. This spreads the batter and makes the crepes very thin. Tilt pan to spread crepes. If there are holes in the crepes, cover with a drop or so of batter. When they are golden, turn crepes over and brown quickly on second side. If crepes are to be sauced later, cover with wax paper to prevent drying. They may be frozen between sheets of wax paper. Makes 28 crepes.

Sauces:

>   1/2 lb. butter
>   2 egg yolks
>   1 cup powdered sugar
>   1 cup grated orange rind
>   1/2 cup orange juice
>   1 jigger Curaçao

1. The sauce may be prepared in the morning. Melt butter in double boiler, add egg yolks, sugar, orange rind and juice and stir, cooking slowly until mixture thickens. Add Curaçao and stir. Remove from stove.

2. Remove crepes from freezer and thaw. Spread sauce lightly over crepes and roll or fold in quarters. If you prefer rolling crepes, slice off the tips to give them a more uniform appearance. Arrange neatly in ovenproof dish and pour rest of sauce over crepes. Warm for short time in 350°F. oven until ready to flame.

The Flame:

When it's time to serve, place platter with crepes on cart or table where individual warm plates are waiting. In a heated chafing dish pour in 1/2 cup 80-proof brandy. When warm, not boiling, light with a match. Appoint an assistant to help you by placing two or three crepes on an individual dessert plate while you spoon flaming brandy over them. When flame dies down— voila! Crepes Suzette!

MY FAVORITE CHRISTMAS DINNER

When a dozen skis and poles are piled up on the front porch like matchsticks; when the stereo belts out the same pop tune over and over; when a borrowed high chair sits in the corner; when the dog barks at the substitute postman; when the cat paws blue and gold pine cones; when the ample house shrinks to half its size, then it's my favorite time of the year—Christmas vacation!

Traditionally we celebrate Christmas Eve dinner with at least twelve to twenty close friends and relatives whose age range may be anywhere from one to seventy-one. The climax of the months of shopping, gift wrapping, labeling and whispering occurs after dinner when a bell is rung announcing Santa's arrival and all the lights in the world seem to glow in the eyes of the smallest believer.

Our seating and menu is also traditional, but this year when we had eighteen guests we made two innovations. First, we set up two tables of nine, one in the dining room for the adults and one in the adjoining study for the young people. Then we set up identical buffet tables in each room, so instead of one enormous turkey, we prepared two medium-size ones along with duplicate platters of vegetables, sweet potatoes, etc. We appointed a junior host and hostess to look after the young folks, a plan which succeeded even beyond our wildest dreams, because one of the three-year-olds announced, "Mother, you can't come in here—we're having our own party!" leaving us gleefully free to enjoy a leisurely uninterrupted meal!

Addenda: We used our oven and portable electric roaster to cook the turkeys; but if you have only an oven, one turkey can be done early in the day, or even the day before and served with hot gravy.

Christmas Dinner Menu

Hors d'oeuvres:

Cold Smoked Salmon,   Baby Swiss Cheese,
Liver Pâté, (see index)
Roast Turkey with Chestnut Dressing, Pan Gravy
Cranberry Sauce
Sweet Potatoes with Marshmallow Cockaigne
Spinach Soufflé
Cloverleaf Rolls
Rum-Fruit Savarin Ring
Christmas Cookies   Nuts
Mocha Coffee

Wine suggestions: Imported—Moselle (young, white, slightly sweet). Serve cold (40°F). White Bordeaux (fairly dry), Serve cool (50°F). Red Margaux (pleasant Bordeaux) Serve room temp. (60°F). Domestic—California Wine. Fairly dry Rhine wine. Serve cold (40°F).

ROAST TURKEY

The second innovation pertains to the special preparation of this year's turkey and forgive me if I sound like a T.V. commercial, but for the juiciest, most delicious turkey you'll ever enjoy, put the dressing under the skin of the breast instead of in the cavity. You see, the tender breast meat is usually done before the tougher legs, and when you stuff the turkey under the skin it helps to correct this imbalance.

Fresh or Frozen?

A fresh turkey is better of course, but not always available. For frozen turkeys, allow 2 hours per pound for defrosting in refrigerator and 1 hour per pound at room temperature.

Chestnut Dressing

You may prepare the stuffing ahead, but always wait to stuff the bird until just before roasting. Use your own favorite stuffing or our favorite chestnut dressing which is made as follows for an 8- to 10-pound turkey.

    1 lb. can chestnut stuffing (domestic or imported)
    4 cups toasted bread cubes
    1/4 cup water or stock
    1/4 cup chopped onions
    2 tablespoons butter or margarine

Place chestnut dressing in a large mixing bowl, add bread crumbs and liquid. Sauté onions in butter and mix everything together lightly. With spoon or your index finger, loosen skin from flesh (you'll meet with a little resistance just at first) and gradually work your hand across the entire turkey breast all the way to the neck and across the top of the drumstick. Now take a handful of stuffing at a time and spread under loosened skin until it is evenly distributed. (Remember the dressing will expand some.) The crop cavity as well as the loose skin of the neck may also be stuffed. If there's any stuffing left, put this in the cavity of the turkey. Close both openings with small skewers, or sew skin together with a darning needle threaded with white string. Tie a heavy knot on the end of a long piece of string and wrap crisscross around turkey taking care to tie wings and drumsticks close to the body. Secure the end of the string with knot on top.

Turkey Paste

> 1/4 lb. butter
> 2 tablespoons honey
> 3 tablespoons paprika

Melt butter, add honey and paprika and rub over turkey. Optional: Cover with a muslin cloth soaked in butter after 1/2 hour and remove cloth 1/2 hour before turkey is done, so it may brown.

Roasting Time

Preheat oven to 450°F. Place the turkey on a rack in an uncovered pan, breast side up and immediately reduce oven heat to 325°F. Baste occasionally; however if you use the muslin cloth you can forget about it as there is no need to baste the turkey.

Figure 25 minutes to a pound for a stuffed bird weighing 12 lbs. For a turkey over 18 lbs. reduce the oven to 300° and allow 20 minutes per lb. (To make stock see pan gravy). A Word About Foil: We do not recommend using foil when roasting because foil traps the steam and gives the bird a stewed taste.

Pan Gravy

This must be made in the roasting pan and not in a skillet! Remove turkey from pan and keep bird warm on platter in oven. Pour off all but 2 tablespoons of drippings and place pan on stove over low flame. Add 1 tablespoon flour and stir until thickened. Add either a 10 1/2-oz. can of chicken consommé or 1 cup turkey stock. (Made from 2 quarts of cold water, turkey giblets, wing tips, neck bone, 1 onion sliced, 2 stalks of celery with tops and several sprigs of parsley. Bring to boil and let simmer for 2 hours. Strain.) Add salt, pepper and stir over low flame for 5 minutes. Optional: You may strain the gravy before serving in your gravy boat.

SWEET POTATOES WITH MARSHMALLOWS COCKAIGNE

Cockaigne is an imaginary country of idleness and luxury— *Schlaraffenland* in Germany.

We always serve a sweet potato casserole topped with marsh-mallows for our Thanksgiving and Christmas dinner because most children, as well as adults, love it. If one cares to fuss, in-stead of serving the sweet potatoes in a baking dish, make indivi-dual baskets by taking an orange and cutting two wedges out of the top half, leaving a little handle. Then remove the meat, and zig zag or scallop the edge of the basket with a sharp knife. Add the following filling and top with half a marshmallow on each side of the handle. Warm in oven until the marshmallow begins to melt but does not brown.

      12 large sweet potatoes
      3/4 cup orange juice
      3/4 cup brown or granulated sugar
      2/3 cup melted butter
      Dash of nutmeg (optional)
      12 marshmallows

Cook unpeeled sweet potatoes in a large pot of boiling water with lid on until tender or for about 25 minutes. Peel while still warm. Preheat oven to 325°F. Put potatoes through a ricer or mash them with a potato masher, or in an electric mixer. Add orange juice, sugar and butter and beat until they are very light. Place in 2-quart baking dish; warm in oven for 15 minutes Just before serving place marshmallows on top about 1/2-inch apart turn oven up to 450° for a few minutes, or until marshmal-lows are lightly browned. Makes 12 servings.

SPINACH SOUFFLE AND VEGETABLES IN GENERAL

The proper timing of cooked vegetables is so important that from my party-going experience, unless one has an expert staff in the kitchen, too many vegetables such as fresh asparagus, peas and sometimes even snap beans are usually overcooked, limp or shrivelled. I must confess that during the busy holiday season with numerous house guests under our roof, I frequently resort to the short cut of serving frozen bought spinach soufflés, of which there are several excellent brands on the market. Thus, I have no last-minute timing to worry about, and I am able to free space in my refrigerator, which is at a premium during the holidays.

I am not above buying frozen peas and green beans. However, I almost always use a shorter cooking time and less water than the package calls for. Then the vegetables stay crisp, moist and retain their color.

For other times of the year when I have more time, I prepare such vegetables as spinach ring cooked in a mold, then filled with sautéed mushrooms, cooked rice or tiny canned, well-drained beets. A carrot ring filled with mushrooms or hearts of artichokes is also a favorite, as is a broccoli ring served with sauce—cheese, onion, or Hollandaise.

Mrs. Nathan Cummings, hostess par excellence, loves to serve an "assemblage" of vegetables at her frequent large gourmet dinner parties in New York and Chicago. Mr. Cummings, founder of Consolidated Food Company, which includes all Sara Lee products, concerns himself with high quality food; Joanne devotes her party planning efforts to splendid presentations. I recall in particular an outstanding arrangement composed of whole cauliflower placed in the center of a round platter, surrounded by shells of unpeeled baked tomatoes filled with purée of spinach, alternated with boats of zucchini filled with purée of carrots.

Vegetables served in cases (green peppers, cucumbers, artichokes, blanched onions, for example) or petit pois served on hearts of artichokes are so much easier to handle and look much more attractive on the dinner plate. Farcies, served by Princess Grace, and other vegetable recipes are listed in the index.

Of all the foods that set a meal apart, it's the garden-variety vegetable that lifts a menu from the "good dinner" class to one of elegance and charm.

RUM-FRUIT SAVARIN RINGS

This recipe makes three savarin rings in 9-inch molds with curved bottoms. I am assuming that you will freeze two rings for later use (how lovely to have a few in your freezer!) and am giving you the Rum Syrup and Fruit Filling for only one ring, enough for ten servings.

Dough for three rings

    1 cake fresh yeast
    1/2 cup lukewarm milk
    4 cups sifted flour
    1 tablespoon sugar

1/2 teaspoon salt
9 eggs
1/2 lb. melted butter

Rum Syrup for each ring

2 cups sugar
3 cups water
1 orange rind, coarsely chopped
1/2 cup light rum

Fruit Filling for each ring

1 pint whipping cream
1/2 cup milk
1/2 package vanilla instant pudding mix
1/4 cup light rum
2 cups fresh strawberries, or peaches, mixed with apricots, blueberries or raspberries

Crumble fresh yeast in warm milk and stir until dissolved. In a large electric mixing bowl, pour sifted flour, sugar and salt. Add yeast mixture. Beat whole eggs and add to dry ingredients. Turn on electric mixer at low speed for 10 minutes. Pour melted butter on top of batter. Do not stir. Cover with a towel and let rise for one hour. Then beat buttered dough again in the mixer at low speed for two minutes. Generously butter and flour three ring molds and pour batter one-third full into molds. Let rise until double. Bake in 400°F. oven for 15 minutes, then reduce heat to 350°F. and bake 10 minutes more. Let cake cool in ring molds; freeze two if desired.

Make rum syrup: Boil sugar, water and orange rind for 15 minutes on top of stove. Add rum and remove immediately from stove. Baste Savarin ring with boiling syrup until soft and puffy. Let cool slowly.

Make Fruit and Whipped Cream Filling: Whip cream. Combine milk and vanilla instant pudding mix and add rum. Before pudding sets, fold in most of the whipped cream, reserving some for decoration. Finally fold in fresh fruits, also reserving a few for decoration. Place rum-soaked Savarin ring on serving platter with curved side up. Fill the center with fruit-rum-pudding mix and decorate the top with whipped cream and whole berries. One ring makes 10 servings.

Dial C for Caterer

"Life is service. The one who progresses is the one who gives his fellow beings a little more—a little better service."

E. M. Statler

There's a dwindling number of glittery people who have the staff—and the Lowestoft—to serve several dozen illustrious guests at a formal sit-down dinner. The "I-never-cater" group is decreasing while elegant entertaining is increasing. People (executive wives, career women, bachelors) who want to dine well—but don't want to cook, are dialing the numbers of reputable caterers to close the small remaining gap left between the automated kitchen and a spangly dinner party.

A caterer may mean anything from a woman who's a fine cook and whose husband happens to own a station wagon, who will prepare and serve a dinner for six in one's own kitchen; to a large, professional catering service with mobile kitchens, which will either wholly or partially prepare and serve a gourmet dinner for several hundred under a heated tent, or for several thousand in a banquet hall.

And one doesn't need to wait for that once-in-a-lifetime occasion—for a 50th birthday or 25th wedding anniversary. Most any caterer will deliver a Quiche Lorraine or a Sacher Torte or whatever you feel like ordering to give your special dinner party that necessary lift.

How does one go about finding a caterer? The best way, of course, is to sample the "cates." (Why did such a lovely, solid word ever go out of fashion?) When invited out, notice if the affair is being catered and if you're impressed, ask your hostess when you call to thank her the next day, if she'll share with you the name of her caterer. A caterer may be recommended by word of mouth or you may do a bit of snooping on your own. I once found an efficient home caterer through a church bake sale; but if you're looking for a large, professional catering service, check the Yellow Pages of your phone book, and then shop around and compare what each has to offer in the way of menus, prices and services, what parties they have catered, how long they have been established. Some caterers serve industry primarily (annual banquets, meetings, conferences, etc.) while others specialize in home functions (weddings, anniversaries, engagements, confirmations and the like), and some do both.

On one of my recent Hawaiian trips, I longed to reciprocate the famous Island hospitality with a cocktail party of my own for about 20 people, so I turned to the phone book and fortunately selected the Gourmet Catering Co. For a little over $1 per person they delivered ice, glasses, platters and chafing dishes filled with seven kinds of hot and cold *pupus* (the Hawaiian name for hors d'oeuvres). The cold marinated shrimp on frilly picks were served in half a scooped-out pineapple shell and, instead of bouquets of parsley, each platter was garnished with fresh orchid blossoms.

Of course, with a bartender the party would have cost more but one of my quiet friends was quite pleased to have something to keep him busy. When I returned the chafing dishes, and equipment the next day, I learned to my surprise that the Gourmet Catering Co. is a division of Spencecliff who run Trader Vic's and prepare six million meals annually for Hawaii's leading chain of thirty restaurants!

On another occasion, when our yacht was docked at the Brazilian Docks in Palm Beach, the dock master put us in touch with a pleasant caterer who arrived on board in his white jacket carrying a black bundle under his arm in which was rolled a supply of assorted chefs knives. In a very short time he re-appeared not with platters of ordinary chips and dips for our dockside cocktail party, but with a flower garden of dainty garnishes shaped out of radishes, carrots, tomatoes, parsnips, cucumbers, parsley and watercress.

THE OLD TEAM SPIRIT

Some caterers will supply everything, including fine linens, china, crystal, extra chairs and tables, and even the floral centerpieces with matching blossoms floating in crystal finger bowls; while others supply only the food and personnel, but they have access to, and experience working with, other members of the party team. This includes people knowledgeable in the art of calligraphy to address invitations, musicians, acousticians, florists, photographers, lighting experts, parking personnel and marquee suppliers.

A good caterer will:

1. Welcome your suggestions and help develop your party so that it reflects your own taste and personality.

2. Use your own recipes and keep them confidential.

3. Supply you with bonded, trained waiters, waitresses, and bartenders.

4. Free you from all responsibilities during and after the party. (They'll even turn out the lights for you after you've retired!)

An experienced caterer will ask for a party-planning conference as described in this letter from Virginia M. McCann, Party Planners of Neiman-Marcus in Dallas, Texas: ". . . briefly given a date, the number of guests, a possible theme—if the host or hostess has one in mind, or the purpose of the party, and an estimated budget—we then develop a plan—whether it be a party, wedding or whatever, and submit this to the client together with the total charges involved. Upon receiving approval, we then execute every detail. The décor, food, help, music or entertainment is booked, invitations are sent—the hostess need only be at the door to greet her guests . . . and pay the bill. We design and build all the special 'sets' that may be called for—sculpt ice or any number of other things—in short anything a party might require, we do, including flower arranging or whatever."

After the conference, all arrangements are confirmed in writing, usually in triplicate: one copy is sent to the customer, one copy is retained by the party consultant and the third copy is passed on to the Head Butler or the person in charge on the premises of the party. Work sheets are sent to the catering kitchen where much of the food is prepared in advance, with additional copies sent along for reference by the cook on the party premises.

A conference with a party consultant should be as honest and aboveboard as any conference between you and your lawyer or your priest. Trust her judgment based on years of experience. Tell her exactly what your budget is, what your facilities are and how many people you plan to invite, and she'll tell you if it's possible and how it can best be done. For example, when the Winnetka Garden Club ordered a large number of box lunches from a caterer, the ladies met early to help pack the baskets and thereby reduce expenses.

I asked Marion Boyle, who's been with Gaper's of Chicago for almost 20 years (and they were founded in 1882!), what qualifications a *dream* customer had to have. This is her reply: "One who knows nothing and trusts you and has the wherewithal to do what's necessary, or an old-timer who knows what she wants and can tell you!"

And what imagination some customers have: The latest trend, for philanthropic institutions at least, is to hold meetings in out-of-the-ordinary places. The Chicago Horticultural Society, for instance, gave a party around blossoming azaleas in the conservatory at Lincoln Park. Seating was a problem, ingeniously solved with little tables of three under a veritable forest of flowering trees and shrubs.

Not lacking in pizzaz was a fund-raising dinner held in the Lion House of the Lincoln Park Zoo. Such exotic locales, of course, present special problems to people like Marion Boyle, but she faces near-disaster with equanimity "every other day." The never-to-be repeated blooper which still brings a smile to her pretty face was the catered luncheon planned in a submarine docked at the city pier. When it came time for the cook to go down the hatch, she was much too broad in the beam and couldn't quite make it! It took several frantic telephone calls to book another cook with the proper measurements in the hip-line—but they did it.

Another challenge for a caterer who frequently caters year in and year out to the same people, in the same group, in the same places, is to stamp each party with individuality. For this reason, a seasoned caterer is obviously receptive to suggestions, new recipes and original menus from his customers, so don't hesitate to discuss your ideas freely and openly.

An individual touch after a formal dinner dance given on a Lake Forest estate in Illinois that surprised and delighted me was to find a chef stationed near the exit on the terrace happily passing out freshly fried doughnut holes. At first we couldn't believe our eyes—was it the moonlight? No, there he was in his tall, white chef's hat, standing over his portable grills, dropping batter as fast as he could and bringing out golden bits of fluff that we gobbled up with childish glee.

Miss Boyle tells me that another touch of individuality that's made a king-size impression with the Cotillion Crowd is to serve hot onion soup in mugs while everyone's waiting for the attendant to bring the car around. Well, Chicago is windy, isn't it?

Seriously—I love this idea and can't wait to try it for those long drawn-out cocktail parties when one secretly wonders if one shouldn't have served something, after all, besides just drinks and hors d'oeuvres. Sending your guests off with a solid cup of hot soup is a neat way to help them bridge the gap between your place and wherever they're headed.

HELP! HELP! HELP!

One question always asked is, "How much help do we need and how many guests can we handle? Not enough help can be disastrous, but too much help can create confusion and inefficiency. One of my pet peeves is attending parties where there is too much help and very little service, because the staff is gathered in the kitchen having a ball of their own, and each one thinks someone else is taking care of the guests. At our big parties at home I always ask one waitress to be stationed near me so that I can signal her to wipe up a spilled drink, or to call a guest to the phone, or to ask the cook to replenish a platter. The ideal amount of help is when each person has a definite assignment, knows what his job is and is kept occupied but not frenzied. At a formal dinner today, a waiter is required for every six guests. One bartender will adequately handle 20 to 30 guests. (Later the bartender will often double as a waiter.)

For a formal buffet dinner, with cautious planning of the menu the ratio may be stretched to one waiter or waitress for every eight guests. The number of dishes that are passed for second helpings must be reduced or combined. For instance, meat, potato balls and gravy bowl placed on one large platter; or a vegetable ring filled with rice; or a noodle ring filled with vegetable. This system allows one platter to do the work of two.

Caterers have pet peeves too, especially when they have to deal with a suspicious woman who thinks everyone is trying to take her for a ride. This story concerns a doctor's wife who engaged a cateress to serve dinner at 7:30 for twelve guests. She was to prepare hors d'oeuvres, soup, duck l'orange, vegetables, wild rice, gravy, dessert and coffee.

The cateress suggested she arrive at 2:00 in the afternoon bringing a prepared dessert with her, but the doctor's wife (who was paying by the hour) said she thought that was too early— four o'clock would be time enough because there would be other help there to get things started. When the cateress arrived at 4:00 o'clock there was no other help around! Quickly and desperately she called a friend to give her a hand and between the two of them they managed to cook and serve a lovely dinner, but she only went twice to that house—the first and the last time!

Robert Leberman, head of Casserole, Inc. in Los Angeles, dreads running out of food—and well he might when he's estimating for 25,000 people at a sitting.

"People at buffets eat in frightening, horrendous quantities . . . and the last six people at a benefit are the chairman of the boards, the president and the party chairman with their wives. When they look at the buffet table for the first time if it isn't full and beautiful, the party is a disaster."

It's not easy to outguess people's appetites. "If you underestimate," sighs Leberman, "you're a bum. If you overestimate, you charge too much. If you hit it right on the nose, you're skimpy." Sad, isn't it?

LET'S TALK ABOUT CATERER'S RECIPES

As the author of syndicated articles on party giving, as a hostess in my own home, and as an active committee member of many organizations giving large, public functions, I have over a period of many years consulted with gourmet chefs and top caterers in New York, Chicago, Detroit, Washington, D. C., Palm Beach, Beverly Hills, Honolulu, London, Hamburg, and other cities. Hearing this, you are probably under the impression that I have a collection of recipes first-hand from these experts that reaches from here to the ceiling! Yes and no.

Yes, I do have recipes, but no, they are not useful in the average kitchen either because the directions are too sketchy, amounts too large, or the procedures impracticable in the home. So I'd rather not waste your butter and eggs by passing them on.

One of my best friends coaxed a recipe for a glamorous chocolate cake from her favorite caterer only to give up after wasting a day and costly ingredients. Why didn't the cake turn out? There are several good reasons. 1) Specialties of the house are treasured like gold—do you blame caterers for not passing them out? 2) Even the best-intentioned professional cooks might leave out a step, just because they assume everyone knows certain things—but of course everyone doesn't! 3) Some ingredients are unknown or unavailable to the average housewife, and 4) The equipment in the professional kitchen is so completely different that it's impossible to give accurate timing directions for baking, beating, barbecuing or reheating dishes. So let's leave the specialties to the specialist and turn to a good basic home cookbook for our party recipes.

Many women like to cook a special dish of their own, even for the largest parties when a caterer is called in to do most of the cooking. If you do prepare one homemade specialty, give it an important place on the menu—an excellent hors d'oeuvre or a showy dessert, are focus points. If you can manage Crepes Suzette or another flambéed dessert, you really will give your party a spectacular finale. You may have to increase the recipe to serve a large crowd. Fortunately, I've never had any difficulty in doubling, tripling or quadrupling recipes, because I *always* take the precaution of writing the increased amounts of ingredients on a separate sheet of paper before starting to cook. It's safer to do your arithmetic in advance, not while you are concentrating on cooking.

PLAN—AND PLAN SOME MORE

Unless you have a professional caterer taking care of every detail, it would be sensible for you to have a "run-through" before any exceptionally large party. Some hostesses don't realize till the last minute that their kitchen facilities are inadequate, the borrowed pan is too big for the stove, the electrical wiring is inadequate for all the cooking equipment plugged into it, etc. Be sure that you test the working order of any stored, infrequently used articles like roaster-ovens, deep fryers, and coffee makers.

It's not unusual for the punctilious host or committee member to request a dress rehearsal dinner, including wines, for special occasions where every dish is carefully tasted and the meal is appraised *in toto* for color, texture and appearance.

Perfect party planning began a year in advance—at least for the party in honor of His Royal Highness, Prince Philip, Duke of Edinburgh. The black-tie dinner held in March, 1966 at the Conrad Hilton Hotel in Chicago, was the flawless culmination of innumerable meetings and conferences on both sides of the Atlantic, but for most women like myself, our plans didn't begin until 3 seconds after we held the engraved invitation in our hot little hands.

What to wear? Long gloves and gowns. Who's going? One thousand beautiful people. Where do we sit? At tables for eight. Will *he* speak to *me*? Yes, indeed, ah-yes, indeed!

PARTY FOR PRINCE PHILIP

Prince Philip spoke to everyone as he circled the room during the brief cocktail hour before dinner asking the gentlemen, "What do you do?" while the ladies murmured "Isn't he handsome," "I thought he was taller!" "He's six feet tall!" "How friendly he seems."

After the cocktail party we descended in specially designated elevators to the Grand Ballroom, where 125 tables were set with two-foot-tall centerpieces decorated with a total of 5000 fresh roses and 2500 twinkling votive lights, entwined with 250 yards of Mediterranean-blue velvet ribbon. Truly impressive!

Before entering the ballroom, every gentleman received an envelope with his name on it, and typed in the enclosed card, the table number for himself and his lady, while a chart nearby gave the location of the table numbers. A heavily embossed gold-tasseled souvenir program with menu lay at each place (don't you love to know what you're eating?) along with a plain white handwritten place card accented with a gilt crown.

We were guided through the princely program by the captivating Mr. John Mills, His Royal Highness's personal toastmaster, dressed in a hunting pink tailcoat, who almost stole the show with his booming announcement: "Pray silence. You have permission to smoke!"

Dinner Menu for Prince Philip

CLEAR GREEN TURTLE AMONTILLADO
Golden Cheese Straws
Relishes

FILET OF PIKE SAUTÉ VÉRONIQUE
Aux Fleurons

Jouvet Pouilly-Fuissé

ROAST BARON OF BEEF
Sauce Perigueux
Petite Chateau Potatoes
Fresh Asparagus Tips Polonaise

Barton & Guestier Pommard

HEARTS OF PALM AND AVOCADO ON BIBB LETTUCE
Oil and Lemon Juice Dressing

CHOCOLATE MOCHA MOUSSE SUPRÊME
Petits Fours
Lady Fingers
Macaroons

COFFEE

ANOTHER ROYAL PARTY

On November 19, National Day in Monaco, Prince Rainier and Princess Grace give an official and very formal banquet in the Throne Room for about 70 guests.

A horseshoe table is set up here with white damask tablecloths and napkins which are woven with the Prince's Coat of Arms. The striking centerpieces are composed of bouquets of bright red carnations interspersed with gleaming silver ornaments and authentic "biscuit de Sèvres" groups of mythological figurines.

At the head of the table high-backed red leather chairs are reserved for the guests, while along the sides, guests are seated on small gilt chairs.

Two alcoves beneath the vaulted ceiling open dramatically into the minstrel's gallery where soloists from the Monte-Carlo National Orchestra play softly during the reception.

Banquet Menu

Pirojsky à la russe
Langouste en Bellevue givrée á la parisienne
Sauce aux herbes
Faisan à la crème Grand Succès
Croquettes de maïs
Haricots verts fine fleur au beurre
Les Fromages
Délice glacé Grimaldi
Corbeille de friandises
Meursault 1957
Chambolle Musigny 1959
Champagne Pommery brut
Déjeuner du Dimanche 19 Novembre

LE BAL MODERNE

Once in a lifetime, perhaps, dream and reality blend in a charming mystical way to create enchantment, and such was the case on the memorable evening of the Bal Moderne.

Take a dream castle—or substitute the Great Hall of the Detroit Art Institute with its arched frescoed ceilings; its walls hung with sixteenth century Flemish tapestries; its numerous Gothic entrances guarded by invisible knights in visible suits of armor. Add forty round tables for ten covered with celadon-green cloths and a gossamer overskirt of silver lamé, each with a 2 1/2-foot transluscent cherub centerpiece gaily lighted from within by amethyst, amber, sky blue and jade bulbs; turn Chicago designer John Applegate loose to decorate the adjoining marble-floored Rivera Court for cocktails and dancing among boxwood hedges topped with papier-mâché white doves; add eight-foot magnolia trees and flood the scene with candlelight from twelve-branch candelabras—and you're off to a pretty good start.

But still not enough for the benefit ball in behalf of the Friends of Modern Art, co-chaired by Mesdames Semon E. Knudsen and E. Llwyd Ecclestone! Serve the finest vintage wines and delicacies to four hundred knights in white ties and their perfumed ladies; add the magic touch of Louis "Satchmo" Armstrong's dance music; invite Tony Martin to serenade the queens of Detroit's "wheeling" society dressed by top couturiers in ball gowns designed to complement the Futurist Paintings on exhibit. Ah! Then you have a winning combination—an enchanting candlelight setting, a glittering gathering, a gourmet dinner with impressive gifts to boot, and swinging music.

Months of hectic planning preceded the spectacular success of the Bal Moderne, which was not only the highlight of Detroit's winter season but, according to Cleveland Amory who was there too, "a statelier event than any New York ball this season." Thirty-three committee members divided the responsibility into fourteen subcommittees as follows: advisory, dinner, entertainment, decorations, tickets, reservations, invitations, publicity, picture, gift, bar, lighting and P.A. system, general services and table seating.

THE PERCY-ROCKEFELLER WEDDING

This was catered for 1000 guests by Gaper's, Chicago.

Menu

Miniature Charcoal-Broiled
Tenderloin Steak on Tiny Buns
Stuffed Mushroom Caps
Water Chestnuts and Bacon with
Soy Sauce and Brown Sugar
Hot Cheese Soufflé with Chutney
Crabmeat Canapé au Gratin
Sliced Chicken Finger Sandwich
(some on Whole Wheat)
Fresh Shrimp Canapé
Rolled Cream Cheese with
Sprig of Watercress
Tiny Puff Shells Filled With Lobster Salad

Bridal Decorated Mints
Fondant-Dipped Almonds
Giant Salted Nuts

Wedding Cake

Coffee from Silver Urns
Punch from Silver Bowls

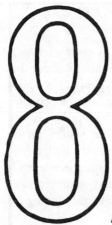

Attention Clubwomen!

*"If you do things merely because you think
some other fool expects you to do them
because he thinks you expect him to expect you to do them, it will end in everybody doing what nobody wants to do, which
is in my opinion a silly state of things."*

George Bernard Shaw in Overruled.

All work and no play makes for a very dull annual meeting
and heaven knows we've been to enough of those!

Interested in persuading people to give their time and dollars?
Anxious to promote a cause? Eager to attract a following? You'll
have a greater success when you underscore your program with
a seasonal, suitable, strong party theme.

Why? Well, for one thing, the more people you involve in
planning, decorating, hostessing and arranging, the more support
and *steam* you generate for your program. Results—better at-
tendance. Secondly, when people arrive and find that someone
has "fussed", they're more apt to participate to a greater degree,
even if it means just listening more attentively to a speaker.
Thirdly, they'll be able to visually recall your program and for
a longer period of time. And lastly the fun of decorating and
creating a magical atmosphere attracts people to your program
who might otherwise never have become involved. All solid reasons for voting for a decorating budget.

BUDGET, BUDGET, WHO'S GOT A BUDGET?

Everybody has a budget!

A good budget must be limited and tailored to meet each person's particular situation, and variations are bound to occur between a budget designed to decorate the school gym for a senior prom or the fraternity house for homecoming or the country club for a private début. But no matter. With willing hands and a little imagination one can achieve spectacular results on an "economy" budget just as well as on an "unlimited" budget.

True, much of the decorating committee's success depends on advance planning; in fact we usually started many months ahead and with luck we even cajoled suppliers into giving us things wholesale.

Two occasions come to mind when we designed a conversational centerpiece for annual charity meetings. On the first occasion we used a "Service Tree" about 18" high, made of irregular pieces of simulated driftwood which we placed in a styrofoam pot. To this tree we attached Grandmother Stover's Miniatures (available in any stationery or department store). We selected these charms to represent various services provided by social agencies to our community. For instance an automobile represented the *Volunteer Driving Corps,* and a tiny pair of eye glasses represented *Aid to the Blind,* a book represented the *Volunteer Library Program* and so forth. When it came time to assemble the additional thirty-nine centerpieces from the original model, we invited a group of Camp Fire girls to complete the job which they did in a few short hours one Saturday afternoon. The girls were delighted to make their contribution to their community organizations.

The second occasion was the celebration of a tenth anniversary of one of our community agencies and for this we used a birthday party theme. We made huge pink crepe paper rosettes for each table and filled the ballroom of a downtown hotel with hundreds of large pink balloons which we inflated with helium and tied in huge clusters around the pillars. The budget for all this, less than $35.00, was absorbed in the price of the luncheon. The decorations quickly helped transform a large dull windowless ballroom into a gay, festive banquet room, and after the luncheon meeting so many agency directors asked permission to keep the conversational centerpieces for their own future meetings, that we initiated the practice of putting a star under one plate at each table; whoever happened to be seated there won the table arrangement.

CREPE PAPER ROSETTES:

Quick, easy and inexpensive to make in quantity, one rosette equals an entire bouquet; they're attractive in any and all colors. The edges can be sprayed with glitter, silver, or gold paint and made weeks in advance; they won't wilt. Change colors to suit the occasion. For example, for *New Year's Mardi Gras* or *Hallowe'en,* use orange crêpe paper, multi-colored sequins glued on. For *St. Valentine's Day,* use white crêpe paper with ready made red hearts, various sizes. They can be used indoor or out among shrubs and trees.

Directions for Crêpe Paper Rosettes:

Take one roll of crepe paper, unroll it and lay it flat on the floor, then fold in half lengthwise. Starting at one end, gather the folded side tightly in both hands forming the stem. As you gather, make a quarter turn until you reach the end of the roll.

Wrap stem tightly with wire or heavy string about 1 1/2 inch from bottom.

Separate the edges and fluff paper.

With both hands, using heel of palm and not finger tips, gently pull crepe paper edges from outside around and around to center. This teasing of the crepe paper gives it a ruffled effect like a carnation or peony. Shake the rosette vigorously and you will have a lovely flower.

For smaller rosettes (about the size of a large cantaloupe), cut the roll of crepe paper in half lengthwise after unrolling it on the floor. Then fold and proceed as directed.

THE RIGHT TIME, THE RIGHT PLACE

When selecting a meeting room or hall there are several important things to remember. Some rooms are easier to decorate than others. For instance, I prefer a room with windows for luncheon meetings, while in the evening one doesn't require natural daylight. Instead, check the draperies for color and pattern. Rooms with mirrors, of course, are usually desirable at night because they reflect color and sparkle.

As a general rule, it's safe to say one can create a smashing effect by following the principle of a three-ring circus and concentrating on decorating three focal areas, 1) the entrance, 2) tables (speakers' table, buffet table and dining tables), 3) the orchestra or bar.

In addition, the room should be checked for the following conveniences. Is there easy access to the kitchen? Is there a platform for the speakers' table? Are there outlets for mikes and lights? What are the fire laws regarding the use of candles and flammable materials? (One may have to clear the latter with the fire department who have been known to station a fireman to standby on special occasions.) And finally, is there convenient parking for guests.

LIGHTS

Decorators have created marvelous effects both indoor and out by using Chinese lanterns or borrowing Christmas tree lights. Of course with the latter, one can use all blue or pink or gold lights or blinking lights to achieve the desired effect.

Or there are times one might prefer using nothing but candle-light to achieve a glamorous effect.

For outdoors, one can use a dozen or more medium-size paper bags filled with three inches of sand, with a candle placed in the sand. Fold the top down to form a cuff outside the bag. When the candle is lighted and the bags are put along a garden path or patio wall or beach, the flame gives off a lovely glow that can be seen at a great distance.

PHOTOGRAPHS, ETC.

Sometimes it's fun to honor a person or an occasion by enlarging a diploma or wedding certificate or a photograph taken from the family album. Any certificate, drawing, or black and white or colored photograph can be blown up as large as 2 x 3 feet and hung over the mantel. (See Sources of Supply.)

For a special birthday or anniversary, how about ordering a full-size front page souvenir copy of the New York Herald published on the very day of one's birth or on one's wedding day? This newspaper is available from the date 1900 through April 24, 1966. (See Sources of Supply.)

TABLECLOTHS

Co-ordinated cloths for card tables, folding metal tables topped with round plywood or hardboard folding circles for various occasions could be club property, or could be rented as needed.

The possibilities for creating pretty party cloths are limitless on even a moderate budget. One can use such inexpensive fun ideas as spreading out a Chinese or Japanese newspaper for an Oriental supper, or taping sheets from old comic books together for a children's party, as we mentioned earlier, using sheet music for a musical theme.

For a graduation party, church or temple sisterhoods can write the name and date of members of the graduating class of Sunday school on an inexpensive white cotton cloth with a black magic marker.

Cloths to fit the menu are always a good idea. For a curried menu, one can use a crewel Indian print spread or a Persian handloomed blocked print. Both are quite reasonable. One can make pretty dainty net cloths for a sweet table as described in Chapter III under Champagne Teas. One can make use of felt, lace, organdy, satin, cotton and denim. One can use gay patterns in prints, checks and stripes. Cloths can be trimmed with rick-rack, French ribbon, fringe and frogs with the trim made into co-ordinated napkin rings. Cloths can be appliquéd.

Has it occured to you to tint those old white linen cloths? Follow the directions on any popular brand package dye sold in department or drug stores. Select any shade you like, mix the dye thoroughly with hot water in your washing machine. Then put the linen, wet, in the machine and presto! It will emerge beautifully tinted. Don't hesitate to dye embroidered linen because it doesn't matter if the embroidery takes on a darker or lighter shade; in fact, it's prettier that way.

No matter how formal or informal the party may be, an appropriate cloth adds a solid impact to the total decorating scheme!

DOILIES:

There my be an occasion when one would like to co-ordinate a lace paper doily with the tablecloth or party theme. This is quite simple to do. Just cut out the center section of the lace paper doily with a scissors and then replace the center with a circle of gift wrapping paper, newspaper, or printed material and glue under the lace border. These doilies can be used under sherbet or water glasses or on platters for cookies.

BALLOONS:

Balloons are available not only in all colors but in various sizes and shapes. They can be ordered ahead with printing and designs. (See Sources of Supply).

Be sure to allow sufficient time to blow up a large number of balloons and corral some willing helpers to pump air into balloons with a gadget made for this purpose or arrange for the use of tanks filled with helium. These can be rented.

SPARKLERS:

Sparklers always create a stir when used on a birthday cake or on the Fourth of July, or just to make an announcement.

HOW TO MAKE A HAWAIIAN FLOWER LEI

Most children who live in Hawaii are quite expert at making flowers leis—it's that simple!

Take a darning needle and some heavy thread and any mainland flowers such as asters, carnations, dahlias, daisies, chrysanthemums, gladioli and draw a needle through the center of the flower adding flowers until the lei is about a yard long. Tie ends together.

Keep leis fresh by sprinkling with water and keeping them in a plastic bag in a cool place until ready to use.

DECORATING COMMITTEE CHECK LIST:

> *paper and pencil*
> *crepe paper*
> *construction paper*
> *poster board*
> *stapler*
> *Scotch tape*
> *glue*
> *magic...marker*
> *ruler or yardstick*
> *scissors*
> *thumbtacks*
> *wire*
> *twine*

PROFESSIONAL PARTY PLANNERS

Many large communities have professional party planners, a comparatively new service which goes far beyond the job the former social party secretary used to perform. There are also several national party suppliers who will gladly mail party accessories (see Sources of Supply). If you don't need it immediately write away for such exotic items as fresh orchids, anthurium, Birds of Paradise and ti leaves along with tissue paper pineapples, Kona coffee, hula records and conch shells which can be mailed on order.

Party Calendar

Fashions zip in and out so quickly nowadays that by the time this book is off the press the current craze may be totally passé, therefore the calendar which follows is designed around more or less permanent themes. But freshness and originality are always welcome, so by all means capitalize on up-to-the-minute trends in creating individual themes for your party.

The Party Calendar

"Time has no divisions to mark its passage, there is never a thunderstorm or blare of trumpets to announce the beginning of a new month or year. Even when a new century begins it is only we mortals who ring bells. . . ."—Thomas Mann

JANUARY — NEW YEAR'S DAY

Not one but three choices!

T. V. Brunch

Early birds and flower lovers invite friends and neighbors to view Pasadena Parade of Roses; give time, date, place, etc.

Invitations: Sketch three roses in parade formation.

Menu: See Chapter II, add chilled rosé wine.

Decorations: A driftwood "tree" centerpiece to which rose corsages or boutonnieres are attached for each guest.

Afternoon

Have an Open House with Holland-Dutch overtones (the custom of calling on New Year's Day was introduced to the U. S. in what was then Nieuw Amsterdam, now New York).

215

Invitations: In the form of a windmill—"Open House: It's an old Dutch custom to celebrate New Year's Day with a Rijsttafel—join us, etc."

Menu: Have a Rijsttafel (see index) featuring shrimp (or veal) curry, cooked rice, exotic dried fruits, Edam or Gouda cheese, dry crackers; or sweet table—rich hot chocolate or cocoa; eggnog, marzipan cakes and Hopjes candy, of course. Do include Lucky Herring salad as a dip; it's an Old World superstition that those who eat herring on New Year's Day will always have money in the year ahead.

Decorations: Dutch shoes as a centerpiece and blue delft ware on the table—tulips from the florist, too!

Evening

Give a small dinner (see Chapter VI) for your closest friends.

Activity: Have each husband write down "the happiest event of the year for us as a couple"—the most embarrassing, the most comic, etc. Have each wife do the same. Score ten for every matched event (where husband and wife both agree). The highest scoring couple wins an appointment book each.

JANUARY 3, 1959 – ALASKA, 49th STATE ADMITTED TO THE UNION

Cocktail Party - *6 o'clock* (a good chance for a couple to entertain "delightfully small" before a large and fashionable benefit dance)

Invitations: Come to our igloo on January 3rd. We're getting things iced up for the Snow Ball! Give time, date, place, etc.

Snow Ball - *7:30 P.M.*
Invitations: Formal engraved.
Dress: Black and white.
Decorations: Hang a sign at the entrance door, "Welcome to Alaska, Land of the Midnight Sun!" Make a gold paper sun or the reflections of sun's rays with skillful use of lights. Use black and white décor with gold accents. For centerpieces use igloos, penguins, spears, walrus tusks or Eskimo masks. Use white styrofoam balls for place-card holders.
Menu suggestions: Alaska Cocktail. (Same as martini except use: 1 part yellow chartreuse to 5 to 7 parts gin.) Alaska King Crab or Salmon. Snow Peas. Iceberg Lettuce Salad with Thousand Island Dressing. For dessert, Baked Alaska or Snow Balls (Chapter II).
Activity: Dancing to a smooth band.

JANUARY 19 – BIRTHDAY OF PAUL CEZANNE
(1839-1906) *French painter and father of modern art.*

Afternoon

Invitations: Use postcards obtainable at most art museum depicting the work of Cezanne.
Decorations: Use red apples for a centerpiece, of course! Pale green cloths. For Moulin Rouge posters, etc., see Sources of Supply.

Evening - Beaux-Arts Bal or Bal Moderne (See Chapter VII)
Dress: Black tie or costumes.
Activity: Have artists make sketches of guests. Dance The Apple Dance: Each couple dances with one apple held between their foreheads. The couple who keeps the apple there longest wins—a good Cezanne print or book to each winner.

JANUARY 24, 1848 –
GOLD WAS DISCOVERED IN CALIFORNIA

Evening - Wild, Wild West Anniversary Party

Invitations: Glue playing card and poker chip on each invitation. January 24, 1848 Gold was discovered in California! January 24, 19?? John marries Julie! So here's a golden opportunity to celebrate our silver anniversary—25 wild years of matrimony. Please join us; give date, time and place, etc. Come dressed as you were 25 years ago!

Decorations: Checked tablecloths, sawdust on the floor. Spray rocks gold to simulate nuggets and use for centerpieces. Serve cold cuts at a "Free Lunch" counter include pretzels and popcorn. Blow up wedding picture; order 25 year old newspaper (see Sources of Supply).

Music: Player piano, singing waiters or Barbershop Quartet. pass out false handlebar mustaches to men.

Activities: Roulette table, dice games, poker, black jack. (Give guests phony paper money to gamble with, and prizes to those who have the most money at the end of evening). Stage a phony holdup. (See Sources of Supply.)

FEBRUARY –
RESORT WEEPERS PARTY FOR STAY-AT-HOMES.

Evening

Invitations: Mail invitations on Palm Beach, Acapulco, or Sun Valley Post Cards saying, "Wish you'd be here on" etc. Give date, place, time, etc. of party.

Dress: Summer sportswear or ask everyone to dress in the native costume of the place he'd most like to be. This will bring out a variety of bull fighters, Hawaiian dancers, ski outfits and bikinis. Over "public address system" announce arrival and departure of airliners and ships from exotic foreign ports.

Decorations: Bright paper flowers (see rosettes). Travel posters. Move garden furniture, umbrellas, folding chairs and swings indoors. Fill sand pails with potato chips, pretzels, etc. Serve frosted rum drinks.

Activities: Dance to "Summertime" music. Play ping-pong, indoor golf and putting games. Set up live fish in an indoor aquarium.

FEBRUARY 12 – LINCOLN'S BIRTHDAY

Evening

Invitations: Make your own invitations by pasting Lincoln-head pennies on a card. Please help us celebrate Lincoln's Birthday on February 12th, give time, place etc.

Centerpiece: Use black stovepipe hat as centerpiece (see Sources of Supply). Invert hat, add container, fill with flowers. Run a ribbon from under hat to each dinner plate. During dinner have guests pull their ribbon one at a time. Attached to the end will be a question such as:

> Q. On what stamp is Lincoln's portrait?
> A. 4¢ stamp
> Q. On what denomination currency is Lincoln's
>   portrait?
> A. $5.00 bill
> Q. Is it full face or profile?
> A. Full face

After-dinner debate: Divide the group into three teams. Present one team with a *pro* and the other team with the *con* of any age-old argument, such as "Should a woman be president of the U.S., yes or no?" But avoid too controversial topics! Limit time for presentation. (The third team acts as jury and rotates so that each group is jury at least once)

Stunt: Supply men with false whiskers as they arrive.

Addenda: Lincoln loved a good joke. When a fat lady accidentally sat on his stovepipe hat he said, "I would have told you that the hat wouldn't fit before you tried it on!" Another time he commented, "My father taught me to work—but not to love it!"

FEBRUARY 14 – ST. VALENTINE'S DAY

Afternoon—Champagne Tea (Chapter III)

Invitations: Traditional hearts and flowers, or cupids.

Decorations: Red velvet and satin accented with white lace.

Activity: A good opportunity for a woman's group to sponsor a spring fashion show (have a lively commentator). Consult with your local dress store. They will co-operate with large groups.

Memo: Hang paper Tiffany lamps (see Sources of Supply).

Evening—Famous Lovers Party, dinner dance.

Dress: Full costume or head-dress only.

Activity: Color one half of a heart pink, the other blue. Tear each heart roughly in half. Give pink to woman, blue to man. Matching halves are dinner partners.

Valentine Dance: One couple starts dancing for a few minutes. The music stops and each person chooses a new partner repeat until everyone is dancing.

Decorations: Lots of red and white balloons and rosettes, candles, paper lace doilies.

Menu suggestions: Heart-shaped molds, candies.

Alternate evening party: Duplicate Bridge session. Write to the American Contract Bridge League 125 Greenwich Ave., Greenwich, Conn. 06830 for *free* literature and information on how to organize a duplicate bridge tournament.

FEBRUARY 22 – GEORGE WASHINGTON'S BIRTHDAY

Tea or House Tour for benefit of historical society—2:30—4:30

Invitation or house tour ads. Glue 13 gold stars in a circle to represent original 13 states.

Decorations: Naturally the early American theme, red, white and blue.

Menu suggestion: See Chapter II for tea ideas. Serve Maraschino Cherry Sauce over pudding or cake slices (see index).

Dinner Dance and Hunt Ball

Decorations: Fox and hounds with fleur-de-lis and eagles from Washington's coat of arms. (George Washington was truly the Country Gentleman who loved to hunt and ride to the hounds. He also loved dancing, hence the Hunt Ball in his honor.)

Dress: Black tie or pink coats. Rent wigs for men, give fans to the ladies (see Sources of Supply).

Alternate: In temperate climates, a river boat party simulating "down the Potomac to Mt. Vernon."

MARCH 11 – COMMEMORATES JOHNNY APPLESEED
(1774-1847). *Patron Saint of the American Orchard, and an early conservationist.*

Morning Coffee—Theme for Annual meetings of Associations of block clubs, conservationists, or beautification programs.

Invitations: Staple a small packet of seeds to a card giving time, place, etc.

Centerpiece: Use a basket of shiny red apples and/or artificial sprigs of apple blossoms on a dark green tablecloth.

Door prize: Jars of apple blossom honey.

Music: Have pianist play "In Apple Blossom Time"

Menu suggestions: Serve chilled apple cider and doughnuts, or see Open Apple Pie (Chapter III).

Memo: Fund-raising event. Engage professional auctioneer whose rapid patter promotes bidding for prizes donated by merchants and friends.

MARCH 17 — ST. PATRICK'S DAY

Evening—Platter Party for young people.

Invitations: Collect old 45-speed records. Cut green paper in 3 1/2″ circle and paste in center giving date, time and place of party. Mail in manila envelope with cardboard backing.

Centerpiece: Use raw potato and ivy. Scoop out huge raw potato (or several) and fill with clump of ivy in soil. This may be done ahead as the moisture of the potato keeps ivy and soil moist. Insert green candle in potato. Use dark green tablecloths.

Menu suggestions: See Corn Beef (Chapter V) or set up a "Do-it-yourself" ice cream bar with assorted flavors and sauces, fruits, toppings, pistachio nuts, mints.

Activity: Invite everyone to bring his favorite disk. Ask a local disk jockey or appoint someone with the gift of gab to program the recordings.

Play Categories: Give each guest paper and pencil and have them write a five-letter word vertically. Across the top name four categories. Guest fill each space with a word whose first letter corresponds with the letter in the vertical column. Give time limit. Score 5 points for each box.

MARCH 21 — FIRST DAY OF SPRING AND JOHANN SEBASTIAN BACH'S BIRTHDAY
German composer, born 1685

Morning Musicale and Luncheon by Women's Music Group
Invitations: See sketch.

Decorations: Spray toy instruments any color and attach paper flowers or fresh flowers set in wet Oasis in openings. See Symphony Luncheon (Chapter II).

Placecards: White card with musical clef.

Memo: Club programs will state the price of the luncheon in the double fold invitation.

Inside:

Spring Musicale

    Monday, March 21
    at 10:30 o'clock
    The Little Club
    Reservations

Reservations	Luncheon
LI 7-6543	12 o'clock
Mrs. Smith	($2.50)

APRIL 1 – APRIL FOOL'S DAY

Evening—Mystery Party!

Invitations: Staple time, place, etc. to a mask or cut colored paper in shape of mask. (If the party is to be held at a club or hotel and the identity of the host is to remain secret, request return address be sent c/o Post Office—Box Number).

Decorations: Cut giant black question marks from poster board and sprinkle with glitter.

Activities: Charter a bus and take the whole gang on a surprise trip to a roadhouse, bowling alley, swimming pool or what you will. Or, engage magicians and comedy waiters, cartoonists for the evening.

Memo: Get trick silverware, etc. from trick store.

Dress: Request ladies to wear paper dresses. Guests may remove masks before dinner is served.

Music: Play the song "Who?" before announcing the name of the host.

Addenda: Giving a "Mystery Party" on someone's birthday or anniversary is sometimes more kind than giving a "Surprise Party". Being surprised robs one of the pleasure of anticipation (and the pleasure of getting one's hair done!)

Evening—Or invite teenagers to an upside-down party.

Invitation: Cut out teenage pictures from magazine and paste them upside down on invitation.

Dress: Wear clothes backwards.

Menu suggestions: Start with cookies and coke, hamburgers and/or pizza and end with a coffee mug of hot soup or tomato juice.

Activities: Show cartoons or home movies backwards. Play games—such as musical chairs—backwards.

APRIL 21 — ROME FOUNDED IN 753 B.C. This day is celebrated in Italy as "NATALE DI ROMA"

Evening—Roman Orgy for a club-sponsored annual ball or several couples may combine in giving this lavish party.

Invitations: Roman letters on parchment scroll tied with purple ribbon.

Decorations: Use purple satin tablecloths with gilded harps entwined with ivy for centerpieces. Scatter reclining garden furniture draped with brightly colored fabric or sheets indoors. Simulate Roman columns and statues. Use torches and braziers outdoors.

Menu suggestions: Large punch bowls. Oyster bar. Long buffet table loaded with whole roasted fowl, roasts, platters of whole fish (bass, salmon, trout). Olives. Serve Caesar Salad, artichokes. Red and white wines. For dessert pass large platters of grapes, figs, dates, pomegranates, and assorted fresh fruit, nuts and cheeses.

Entertainment: Professional juggler or magician.

Dress: Togas, sandals. Provide men with laurel wreaths. Ladies with flowers.

Music: One or more harps and violins.

Memo: Ancient Romans made parsley garlands to hang around their necks, thus preventing intoxication!

APRIL 23 — WILLIAM SHAKESPEARE'S BIRTHDAY, 1564, *English poet and dramatist.*

Matinee—Theater Party
  Invitations: Facsimile of theater ticket.
  Activity: Charter bus to drive young people to theater. Serve refreshments, box lunch (see Chapter II).
Evening
  Invitations: Let's "Ham" it up together for Willie Shakespeare.
  Decorations: Theatrical masks.
  Menu suggestions: Baked Ham with Lima Beans and Pear Casserole, (see Index).
  Activity: Let guests give short excerpts of readings from Shakespeare's plays with modern ad-libbed translations. Have several copies of his works available for reference. Provide wigs, scarves, swords, etc. for props.

MAY 1 — KENTUCKY DERBY CHURCHILL DOWNS, *Louisville, Kentucky*

Noon—Usually given by a group or club for fun or fund-raising.
  Invitations: Red and white checkered card. See sketch.
  Decorations: Red tablecloths with horseshoe flower centerpieces and silk banner "Good Luck".
  Menu suggestions: See index for My Favorite Barbecue.
  Activity: Form a betting pool. Each guest picks a horse in the Kentucky Derby race to win, place or show. Give prizes.
Evening
  Rent horse-racing films from movie rental service. Give guests play money (see Sources of Supply) to bet with at pari-mutuel windows. Sound bell at start of race. Print tickets in advance for each race, win, place, or show with numbers from 1-8 for each horse.
Music: Play "In My Old Kentucky Home" and other Stephen Foster melodies.

Digestive Track Run Down
1 **Mint Julep**
      cool at the start!
2 **Merry Go Round Pie**
      no long shot!
3 **Cole Slaw**
      may be a toss!

4 ***Tomato Pudding***
  sure to come out of the red!
5 ***Chicken Bar-B-Que***
  usually well done!
6 ***Dilli Bread***
  good track record!
7 ***Cheese Pie***
  carries added weight!

MAY 5 — ARBOR DAY

Morning Coffee or Lunch to plant the New Garden Center.
For Garden Club Members
  Invitations: See Sketch.
  Activity: Rake, dig, plant, prune, spray.
  Music: Classical. Attach extension cord to hi-fi speaker and
place outdoors.
  Menu suggestions: Planter's Punch (Chapter IV)
      Sandwiches (Chapter III)
      Dessert: Serve fruit ice cream in paper
      cups set in small clay flower pots. Place
      a real flower (a small geranium maybe)
      in the center.

Now Dig This!
  Dress Sloppy
    Come Early
    Bring Tools
    Work Fast
    Stay Late
      Drink Planter's Punch etc.
      Eat Garden Variety Sandwiches
      and be Merry!

MAY — MOTHER'S DAY. SECOND SUNDAY IN MAY

Noon—Co-hosted by all grown or married daughters and daughters-in-law. (A grand opportunity to celebrate for mothers who avoid celebrating birthdays.)

Invitations: Send snapshot of mother occupied in her favorite activity and follow through on that party theme: bridge or bingo, painting or ping-pong, tennis or boating. Give date, time and place (give party either at mother's, son's or daughter's home; or a public or private picnic ground where small children can run) etc.

Decorations: Mother's favorite flowers.

Menu suggestions: Have each person prepare one course.

Activity: Prepare poems, songs, skits.

Memo: Invite mother's closest friends too!

MAY 30 — MEMORIAL DAY

Flapjack Breakfest or Barbecue Supper

Invitations: Staple a card giving time, place, etc., on a swatch of a bandana or a whole bandana.

Decorations: Gingham tablecloths, kerosene lamps, miniature wagons filled with cacti. Instead of numbers for tables, use cards with brands such as Diamond T, Circle C, Double U, etc. Paint a farm wagon orange and use it as the buffet table. Twine yellow artificial roses around wagon wheels. At night use spot lights. (See Sources of Supply.)

Breakfast Menu suggestions: Flapjacks, maple syrup, butter, bacon, sausage, fresh fruit and berries. Serve outdoors.

Evening—Barn Dance

Menu suggestions: Margarita, Bob's Bar-b-qued Beefsteak, Homemade Corn Relish, Pecan Rolls, (see Index for all recipes).

Dress: Blue jeans and gingham.

Music: Old-time fiddler.

Activity: Pitch horseshoes.

Entertainment: Lasso demonstration.

JUNE 11 — KAMEHAMEHA DAY. Birthday of the first king of Hawaii, celebrated with parades, floats and pageants.

Morning—Kona Coffee

Invitations: Staple the date, time, place, etc. to a paper lei and mail in a box wrapped in Hawaiian print paper (see Sources of Supply).

Decorations: Make an Island scene with miniature palm trees, grass shacks, out-rigger canoes, dolls, ukeleles, etc. Use Hawaiian print cloths or attractive brown and black batik paper goods (see Sources of Supply).

Menu suggestions: See Chapter II.

Music: Play Hawaiian records.

Evening:—Luau

Seat guests on straw mats spread on the ground. Place folding card tables or aluminum tables 8″ off the ground.

Menu suggestions: Beachboy Screwdriver, Pineapple Chunks, Bar-b-qued Spareribs, Sweet 'n' Sour Pork Chops, or Curried Shrimp (see Index for recipes).

Musical Setting: Ukuleles. Hawaiian torches and hula dancers!

Memo: One can be terribly extravagant and order fresh flower leis, anthurium, ti leaves, bird of paradise flown in direct from Hawaii (see Sources of Supply). Give them the *Date of the party and* they will ship them to insure delivery the day before. Write to the *Hawaii Visitors Bureau*, 2051 Kalakaua Ave., Honolulu, Hawaii for information about where to order party materials.

JUNE 23 — *Midsummer eve occurs near the time of the summer solstice, the great turning point in the sun's career. Shakespeare's MIDSUMMER NIGHT'S DREAM is based on the ancient festival celebrated throughout Europe with bonfires.*

Evening—After dusk in the garden.

Invitations: Handwritten on torn parchment in old English script.

Decorations: String Christmas tree lights in trees and shrubbery. Hang Christmas tree icicles from branches to give dreamy effect (see Sources of Supply). Use eerie green and blue spot lights or insert candles in paper bags filled partially with sand.

Use fairy dolls (King Oberon and Queen Titania) as centerpieces surrounded by candlelight and flowers.

Music: Engage strolling minstrels or madrigal singers dressed in 16th century costumes.

Entertainment: Contact local little theater group or University Drama Department to stage one act play.

Menu suggestions: Martini Punch Bowl. Raw vegetable bouquet, onion trees, marinated mushrooms, hot prunes wrapped in bacon, smoked ham. Lima Bean and Pear Casserole, Dobos Torte (see Index for recipes).

JUNE — FATHER'S DAY. THIRD SUNDAY IN JUNE.

Breakfast—Crown Dad King for the Day!

Menu suggestions: Eggs Volcano or Caviar Omelet. See Chapter II.

Symbol of the Day: The rose.

Activity: Plan a family cook-out (Mother does the barbecuing); a picnic, fishing trip, boating excursion, or order tickets for the ball game; help him with a pet project. Present him with a scrap book of his achievements.

Evening:

If you take him out to dinner—don't let him pick up the check!

If you stay home, prepare his favorite food, and pass him a good cigar after dinner.

Family Activity: Show *his* home movies or color slides. If the children are away—invite other Dads for dinner and rent a travel or hobby film or arrange a poker game.

Decorations: A gold crown filled with roses.

JULY 4 — INDEPENDENCE DAY

Noon—Pool party or picnic for young and old!

Invitations: Glue miniature American flags on folded invitations. Surround with gold stars in shape of number 4.

Decorations: Order a patriotic kit (see Sources of Supply) and/or make own firecracker centerpieces. To make firecrackers of assorted sizes, use red, white and blue construction paper. Staple paper into the shape of a cylinder or use rolls which held paper towel etc. In matching-size plastic lids, make a dollar-size hole, pull a coil of heavy red, white and blue wool yarn partially through hole, cut yarn, place lid on cylinder and presto! you have an attractive firecracker.) Use red and white striped tablecloths, blue cornflowers.

Menu suggestions: Iced orange tea, Chapter III.
       Turkey salad, Chapter II.
       Fudge Cake, Chapter III.

Evening—Get-together before or after firework display.

See Chapter V or Chapter VI.

Activities: Invite guests to give a 2-minute humorous campaign speech either for the office of President of the U. S. or local dog-catcher! Have a soap-box handy. Gift wrap bars of soap for souvenir prizes. Or play comedy records. Or organize a baseball game, or sing songs around a camp-fire.

Memo: Use sparklers and torches at night.

JULY 14 — BASTILLE DAY, NATIONAL FRENCH HOLIDAY

Evening—"Saucisson-Vin Rouge" Party

Invitations: A french poodle holding the French flag (see Sources of Supply). Colors: red, white and blue.

Decorations: Put a few chairs and tables, garden umbrella in front of the house on the sidewalk or make a sign over the front door *Cafe de la Paix*. Decorate the tables with miniature Eiffel Towers, Arc de Triomphe, decorate walls with French posters and pennants, use paper table accessories with French motif. (For towers, arc, posters, pennants and paper goods, see Sources of Supply.) Irises for flower arrangements.

Menu suggestions: Serve a great variety of saucisson (sausages), some hung, arranged as artistically as a still-life. Serve vin rouge

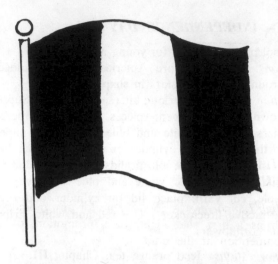

(red wine) preferably Beaujolais in earthenware pitchers and coarse country bread with slabs of butter. A variety of cheeses is optional, along with a luscious green salad such as Camembert Salad a la Rothschild (see index). A big basket of fruit, melons and strawberries are the right finishing touches.

Music: Play popular French records by Maurice Chevalier, etc., or dance to a combo.

Activity: Show travel pictures or art films. Or plan a make-believe cruise down the Seine on a boat. Provide sketch pads for each person to do self-portrait.

AUGUST — SECRET DESIRE PARTY!

Evening

Invitations: Mail flat key with tag attached giving time, date, place, etc. On reverse write, "The key to open the door to your personality! Come as the person you'd most like to be!"

Decorations: Sketch keys of all kinds on poster board: old keys, padlocks, etc. For centerpiece on table make a mobile of assorted keys and locks. These could be sprayed any color. Create dreamlike effects by draping large pieces of gauze around room and spotlight these with blue and green lights (see Sources of Supply). Hang reproductions of Dali paintings.

Dress: Wear the outfit of the person you'd most like to be! or cut keys out of poster board, attach both ends with ribbon to hang around one's neck. Have guests write, "My secret desire is. . . ."

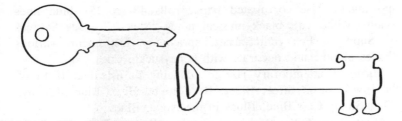

AUGUST 19 – NATIONAL AVIATION DAY AND ORVILLE WRIGHT'S BIRTHDAY 1871.

Flying High Luncheon—A good theme for any momentous occasion such as a first solo flight, or a promotion, or winning a sports competition at the club.

   Invitation: Follow tradition by cutting off a 6″ piece of shirt-tail and writing the date of the solo flight, type of aircraft, and number with a magic marker. Staple this to a card giving date, time, place, occasion etc. of party.

   Decorations: There are many choices of aviation themes including balloons, parachutes, Zeppelins, gliders, autogyros, rockets, jets and space ships. For tablecloths, use green sectional charts (card-table size). Make centerpiece with feather flower arrangement. Put sign over bar—Mixture Control 80 to 100 octane Kerosene additives available. Place a tire on the front walk and tie a rope from the tire to the house as a "tie down" for plane.

   Menu suggestions: Could be anything from a Lindy sandwich to a goose dinner.

   Music: Play "The Magnificent Men in Their Flying Machines!"

   Prizes: Vacation Fly-inns Directory.

   Addenda: (There are a great many other famous first aviation dates. Check your Almanac under *Famous firsts,* aviation.)

AUGUST – AFRO-AMERICAN JAZZ FESTIVAL

Evening

   Invitations: Cut out a musical note from blue construction paper, double. Use inside fold for invitation. "Dig this crazy sound, man!" Give time, date, place, etc.

   Dress: Sharp.

   Decorations: Combine all shades of blue from the palest blue to the deepest purple for tablecloths and background. Use blue spot lights. Use corrugated paper rolls 48″ x 25″ blue lines against white with black musical notes "Melody". (See Sources of Supply.) For centerpieces, spray toy instruments various shades of blue and decorate with honeysuckle vines.

Music: Contemporary jazz for dancing or listening. Birth of the Blues, Basin Street Blues, Born to be Blue, Blue Monday, When Sunny Gets Blue, Blues in the Night, Blues.

Menu suggestions: Barbcued Chicken, Rice with Peanuts, Cole Slaw, Peach Cobbler (see Index for recipes).

SEPTEMBER – FIRST MONDAY – LABOR DAY OR HARVEST FESTIVAL

German Bierstube!—Start anytime of day and just keep it rolling!

Invitations: Write on a white card in green ink, "Ein Prosit! Elbow-bending with German Gemütlichkeit" and give date, time, etc., or see Sources of Supply for Bierstube informals.

Decorations: God's great outdoors is more than enough! Use checked tablecloths trimmed with ivy, cedar or pine. For centerpieces use leafy green and red cabbages. Roll leaves down and decorate with roses. (Keep flowers fresh by placing stems in individual plastic tube available from your florist). For indoors, use Bierstube wall panels 5' x 25', posters and coat of arms.

Costumes: Tyrolean hats, vests, suspenders, aprons are available.

Music: An OOM-PAH-PAH German brass band playing lots of polkas for dancing. Or order Marv Herzog's records with lyrics enclosed.

Activity: The schnitzelbank song is a must! For sheet music, chart, instructions, pointers see Sources of Supply.

Menu suggestions: Serve chilled beer on draught or in a pitcher with pretzels and sauerkraut of course! (An annual event may be inaugurated by organizing an assembly line to slice cabbage and put it in crocks to ferment, then invite the same group back next year to sample the results.) Serve bratwurst, knockwurst, potato salad, cole slaw, apple strudel (see Index for recipes).

Memo: Order booklet with recipes, "How to have a Bierstube" (see Sources of Supply).

SEPTEMBER – LOBSTER COOK-OUT OR SHIPWRECK PARTY

Noon

Invitations: Write time, place, etc. on paper lobster bibs.

Decorations: Fishnet tablecloths over coral, shiny vinyl petticoats. Sea shells and starfish surrounding bowl of live tropical fish. Supply guests with sand pails for lobster shells.

Activity: Boating, fishing, ping-pong, tennis, sun-bathing, swimming, nature walk.

Evening—Treasure hunt on the beach.

Invitations: Affix gold chocolate coin to each invitation. Use black paper and white ink. Or mail invitation in a bottle! Red, black and silver colors.

Activity: Give guests false mustaches; bandanas, eye patches, earrings, pirate hats to wear; supply a map with X marking the spot where the refreshments are to be found!

Music: Harmonica players would be popular now, especially around a bonfire!

SEPTEMBER 16 – INDEPENDENCE DAY IN MEXICO

Cocktail-supper Fiesta

Invitations: Sprinkle a spoonful of confetti in an envelope and write invitations on yellow paper with green ink.

Decorations: Welcome your guests with a sign "Bien venido, amigas, amigos." Decorate the front door with a Mexican tin mask against a turquoise background. Cover the tables with a black cloth trimmed with a red, white and green border or use striped beach towels trimmed with fringe. Use Mexican pottery or pre-Columbian figures with chunky candles accented with gardenias, camellias or roses. Or float poinsettia blossoms (known in Mexico as the flame leaf) in a shallow dish.

Dress: Informal. Supply men with sombreros and ladies with mantillas or flowers and fans.

Music: Hire a marimba band or a flamenco guitarist or play mariachi recordings.

Toast: Salud amor y pesetas para gastarlos! (Good health, love and money, forever!)

Menu suggestions: Margaritas, Mexican Broad Beans and Pepitas for nibblers. Tamale Pie, Mocha Marshmallow Mousse, Coffee Kahlua (see Index for recipes).

Activity: Hang a piñata (hollow paper fish bird, pig, etc.) from ceiling. Blindfold several guests and give them sticks. When they break the piñata, souvenir gifts fall to the ground for everyone. See Sources of Supply for Mexican party accessories.

OCTOBER, ANY DAY INCLUDING OCTOBER 12, COLUMBUS DAY

Evening—Wine Festival

Invitations: Grape festival informals available or draw grape clusters on cards.

Decorations: Let your guests pass through a grape arbor at the entrance. For indoors, use grape garlands, posters, wall panels 4' x 25', lanterns, candles, etc. On the tables use sparkling lamé cloths (paper or cloth) heaped with mountains of grapes. Accent with wicker bottle candles, (see Sources of Supply).

Music: Find an Italian organ grinder (with or without monkey!) or play Neapolitan songs.

Menu suggestions: Hard-cooked eggs—remember Columbus's famous egg debate? (When Columbus was told by a cynic that anyone could have discovered the New World, he placed a hard-cooked egg on the table and asked the room full of noblemen if any could make the egg stand on end. When all failed, he cut off the egg's tip and easily stood the egg on the flat surface. With typical showmanship he said, "Once accomplished, it seems so easy!") Raw vegetable bouquet, Spaghetti, Spinich Salad, Italian Hard rolls, Spumoni ice cream, Bel Paese cheese and crackers. (For free wine tasting booklet, see Sources of Supply)

OCTOBER 31 – CHARLES ADDAMS PARTY – HALLOWE'EN

After Dark!

Invitations: Sketch spiderweb on invitations. Give time, date, place, etc.

Decorations: Use corrugated paper rolls (45" x 25") in grey rustic stone wall design. Hang vampire bats, spiders from ceiling. Use paper Tiffany lights and/or chunky black candles and white tapering candles around the room. (How to make spiderwebs. Nail 6 nails or tacks in the shape of a hexagon to a wall, any dimension you choose. Wrap twine criss-cross from nail to nail then tie twine in circular fashion knotting as you go along, forming a spiderweb. See Sketch. Spray with liquid starch. Let dry and repeat several times. Remove nails and spiderweb will stand alone.) Make charcoal sketches of bats, octopus, skeletons or skulls and place in frames over existing pictures on walls. Make giant spiderwebs and attach to corners of room. For tablecovers, use shiny black vinyl accented with gleaming silver 5-branch candlebra. On buffet tables use Raw Onion Trees, see index. For centerpiece use small trunk or chest, tin or copper-lined, fill with crushed ice for celery, carrot sticks and black olives.

Music: The choice is broad—organ music, electronic tapes, classical or pop. Include "That Old Black Magic" for dancing.

Activity: A billiard table is ideal or it might be fun to scatter small tables around the room set up with chess boards, Chinese checkers, backgammon, etc.

Menu suggestions: A midnight buffet with lots of seafood including an oyster bar, clams or snails, caviar, budget permitting. Or Beef Steak Tartare and cheese, Cafe Royal; (see Index for recipes).

NOVEMBER 3 — BUNKA NO HI Culture Day in Japan.
All those who have contributed to the world of literature, science, art, sports and government are honored with cultural awards on this day.

Afternoon—Japanese Tea 2:00 to 4:00 P.M. sponsored by a Service Group.

Invitations: Choose Oriental informals.

Decorations: Corrugated paper rolls 48" x 25' are available in dogwood blossom pattern or bamboo. Use posters, Japanese lanterns, parasols, pagodas.

Music: Play recordings of Madame Butterfly, the Mikado, Japanese Sandman. For Japanese records, see Sources of Supply.

Menu suggestions: Rice, ginger, almond or fortune cookies, honey cakes, ginger candy. lychee nuts, tangerine slices. Serve tea in Japanese bowls.

Activity: A good opportunity for large service groups (Hospital Auxiliaries, Central Volunteer Bureaus etc.) to give awards to volunteers for the year with a certificate, pin or charm at a special meeting.

Memo: Give Japanese fans for souvenirs. Burn incense.

Evening—Geisha Party

For a small group, surprise guests by renting kimonos, happi-coats, straw slippers, fancy head-dresses for everyone. Provide a dressing room for both men and women along with plenty of make-up. Convert a room or a heated garage into a Japanese teahousè. Use straw mats on the floor and cushions. A door placed across a pair of low coffee tables or bricks makes a perfect dining table. Invite your guests to sit on the floor and provide them with chopsticks. Order a meal from a Japanese restaurant or serve Japanese crabmeat, butterfly shrimp, marinated mushrooms, or cubed beef over Hibachi, Rice and Spinach salad; (see Index for recipes.) Serve warm Sake in tiny bowls.

NOVEMBER – NATIONAL (AND CHILDREN'S) BOOK WEEK (*dates vary annually*)

Luncheon—usually sponsored by the Friends of the Library, Community Centers, etc.

Invitation: Mail in form of a book mark with John Masefield's quote "The days that make us happy make us wise."

Decorations: Place a centerpiece on each table which portrays the title of a current best seller. Example: for the Bible, re-construct Noah's Ark with all the animals. Before guests are seated give each person a slip of paper and pencil with which to jot down their guesses. Give prizes to those who guess each book title correctly.

Menu suggestions: Match menu to the book currently at the top of the best seller list if possible. Example: Michener's "Iberia" suggests Spanish food. Morris *The Naked Ape* suggests bananas, etc.

Activities: Have a Children's Book Fair where people may order or purchase books for young people for holiday giving.

Alternate date: National Library Week. April. (date varies)

NOVEMBER – THANKSGIVING FOOTBALL PARTY – 4th THURSDAY

Afternoon

Invitation: See sketch.

Decorations: Football balloons, pompons, pennants. Colors: earthly tones, rust, brown, green and gold.

Menu suggestions: Set up an hors d'oeuvres table in the form

of a football field, using green felt cloth marked off with 5"
white yardlines. Make a miniature pair of goalposts at each end
from breadsticks and surround field with cheese, crackers,
sausage, etc. Use toothpicks with miniature pennants. Make individual football players out of black and green olives, cocktail
onions, grapes, bits of cheese, pickles. Place tiny numerals on
each player. Menu: Turkey dinner, see Index.

Activity: Set up more than one TV so everyone can watch both
games. Make up a pool and bet which team makes the most
touchdowns in each quarter and/or which team will win and
give the score. Award silly prizes to the winners. In warm
climates organize a game of touch football.

Alternate Date: Any football weekend.

DECEMBER

The entire sentimental month of December usually climaxes
the year's festivities with a medley of family gatherings, debuts,
engagements, home-comings, dances, club parties, church parties
and nationality parties. In bikini climes the December holidays
may be celebrated pool-side or dock-side, while in furry climes
activities are frequently centered inside or hearthside. North or
south, wherever one lives or whatever one's age or status, people
become caught up during this month with the "let's give a party"
spirit. Here are a few popular ideas for holiday entertaining during the jolly season!

DECEMBER 6 – ST. NICHOLAS DAY

Children's Party Tour (for Scouts, Camp Fire Girls and Y
Groups.)

Invitations: Ask each youngster to bring or make a gift to be
donated to a charity.

Menu suggestions: Hot chocolate and Christmas cookies.

Morning Coffee—Good for Office Party!

Invitations: Interoffice memo: Subject: Coffee Break. All fe-
male staff members are requested to bring a plate of Christmas
cookies with recipe. All male employers and employees are directed to taste same. Give date, time, etc.

Christmas Tree Decorating Party

Invitations: Come help us trim our tree
Outside for all to see
When we're done
We'll have fun
With a "nip" and song—R.S.V.P.!

Menu suggestions: Eggnog, Wassail Bowl. Broken Leg.

Activity: Group may help decorate the grounds of several neighborhood homes, each one with a different motif, i.e., one old-fashioned, one modern, one for children. Group then sponsors a Christmas Walk to raise funds for the church, mission or U.N.I.C.E.F., etc.

Or: Newlyweds can invite family and friends to help trim the tree and ask each person to contribute one hand-made ornament.

Home-Coming Party for Young People

(see Devonshire Tea, Chapter III. Platter Party, St. Patrick's Day, Party Calendar).

December 24th or 25th

Christmas Dinner (see Index).

December 31

New Year's Eve. (see Index).

MOVABLE FEASTS AND HOLIDAYS, (dates vary).

January—February

Chinese New Year date depends on the constellation of the moon.

February—March

Mardi Gras falls on the day before Ash Wednesday marking the end of the carnival season. Turkey Gumbo (see Index).

March—April

Purim; Jewish Passover.

April

Palm Sunday, Easter Sunday (see Chapter III for Easter Tea).

September

Labor Day. First Monday. (see Party Calendar).

September—October

Rosh Hashana, Yom Kippur.

October

Aloha week. Dates vary on each Island in Hawaii. (see Party Calendar).

November

Election Day. Second Tuesday.

Thanksgiving. Fourth Thursday. (see Party Calendar).

December

Hanukkah Jewish Festival of Lights. Date depends on the constellation of the moon.

Sources of Supply

Airlines and Travel Agents
Foreign-country posters.

Bazaar Francais, 666 Sixth Ave., New York, N. Y. 10010
Bundt forms; other gourmet cooking utensils including omelet-making equipment.

Bronner's, Frankenmuth, Mich. 48734
Write for party accessories list. Christmas supplies available all year. Corrugated paper rolls, hand-painted murals, Christmas tree icicles, colored lights, pagodas, musical notes, smorgasbord accessories, Japanese records.

Classified Telephone Directory
Check local lists for Party Supplies, Favors and Souvenirs, Window Display Materials and Costumes—Masquerade and Theatrical.

242

Colonial Garden, 270 West Merrick Rd., Valley Stream, N. Y.
Plate warmer and complete catalog of cooking equipment etc.

Department Stores
Head of window displays can supply information about local sources for party goods. In some communities it's possible to rent even a full-size elephant for a circus party.

Florists
Large standards for flowers, decorative fences and screens, etc.

Foreign Consulate
Can sometimes supply material for local color. (I once borrowed an authentic French peasant costume for an April in Paris Party through the Alliance Francaise.)

Hammacher Schlemmer, 147 East 57 Street, New York, N. Y. 10022
Imprinted plastic containers; omelet pans; Scottish smoked salmon; Kikkoman Teriyaki marinade.

Hardware Wholesalers, Inc., P.O.B. 868, Ft. Wayne, Ind. 46801
Swinging grill.

Jordan's Old Virginia Smokehouse, P.O.B. 324, Richmond, Va. 23202

Hobi Inc., Delaware Drive, Lake Success, N. Y. 11040
Spotlights.

Maytag Dairy Farms, Box 506, Newton, Iowa 50208
Blue Cheese Wheel.

Miles Kimball, Oshkosh, Wisc.
Bundt forms, party supplies, etc.

PaPoose Products Co., Inc., 82 First St., Gretna, La. 70053
Zatarain's Gumbo File—your grocer can order it from them.

Paradise Products, Inc., P.O.B. 568, El Cerrito, Calif. 94530
Full-color catalog describes supplies for varied party themes: Smorgasbord, Moulin Rouge, Geo. Washington's Birthday, French, Mexican, Japanese, Pagoda, Hawaiian. Party accessories: roulette table, stovepipe hat, paper Tiffany lamps, etc., Japanese records.

Sally's, 200 North 1st Street, Minneapolis, Minn. 55401
Catalogue of party materials; spiders; bats, etc.

Spencer Gifts, Spencer Building, Atlantic City, N. J. 08404
Enlargements of photographs, certificates, souvenir copies of New York Herald Tribune.

Sunset House, 104 Sunset Bldg., Beverly Hills, Calif. 90213
Front page copies of old newspapers; catalog.

Wine Advisory Board, 717 Market St., San Francisco, Calif. 94103
Recipes for wine tastings, free booklet.

Index

245

NOTES